CW01521840

Danger

by

Harry Ball

Published by
Silver Quill Limited
192 King's Road
Harrogate
HG1 5JG

First edition October 1997

ISBN No: 1 872939 40 6

Copyright
Silver Quill Limited 1997

A Dangerous Game
by
Harry Ball
Harrogate

Published by

Silver Quill Limited
192 King's Road
Harrogate HG1 5JG

First edition October 1997

ISBN No: 1 872939 40 6

By the same author:

Two Brothers at War
Published by
Janus Publishing Company
London, 1992
ISBN Number 1 85756 016 7

Unfortunately Two Brothers at War is out of print.
This book, therefore, has reprinted some material
and photographs from the original book.

Dear Reader

This book is one of many personal stories about P.O.W. life.

As I am in my seventies, my memory is not as good as it used to be. But some experiences can never be forgotten, and these, from many years ago, are still crystal clear today.

I was accepted into the R.A.F. in 1941, as aircrew under training, after failing to be accepted four times, because of my age, and that I wasn't tall enough. Eventually I passed out as a Sgt Wireless Operator Air Gunner (Wop/Ag) at the end of 1943. I did my first trip in January 1944, and was shot down in March 1944.

On the few operational trips our crew managed to do we had a lot of bad luck. Two of the crew I was a member of were killed on our first trip because we ran out of petrol. Five bailed out but because we were so low two of the parachutes failed to open in time. We were at about 500 feet when we jumped, and landed almost on the squadron itself.

A few Op's later we were over Berlin at about 22,000 feet when we were attacked by a German fighter and that was the end of my flying.

Although I was only a prisoner for fourteen months, we did a lot of travelling, by private car, train from Berlin to Frankfurt, cattle trucks from Frankfurt through Poland to East Prussia, a place called Heydekrug, then we marched over the river Elbe. On our way back to freedom, we travelled by truck over the Elbe. We were also on the forced marches towards the end of the war, and released by the 8th Army.

This is my story.

1435132
w/o H Ball
Wop/Ag

August 1997

THE CREW
Mcdonagh (Canadian Bomb Aimer), Collingwood (Scots, Rear Gunner),Whitelaw (Scots, Flight Engineer),Van Slyke (Canadian, Pilot and Skipper), Ball (Wop/Ag), McGillivary (Canadian, Navigator), Grant (Scots, Mid Upper Gunner).

HARRY BALL in 1996

PREFACE

This book has been written by Harry Ball, and it is in two parts. It is the second book to be written by Harry about his part in the Second World War.

The first was his autobiography about his life of some seventy years, entitled "Two Brothers At War". It was written mainly for his family, but after publication it received much local acclaim and approaching 1000 copies have been sold to date. Many copies have been sent to addresses around the world, and some to historical and military reference libraries.

Unfortunatly "Two Brothers at War" is now out of print, so the opportunity has been taken to include some material already published, where it is appropriate. This book is all about five years experience in the R.A.F. as a Wireless Air Gunner in Halifax bombers, and what it was like as a prisoner of war in Germany. The first part of the book carries the same description as the main title - A Dangerous Game - and covers the remarkable detail still carried in Harry's mind of months on an Operational Squadron in 1944. Life expectancy on a Squadron was not great.

The second section Harry has called "An unwilling guest of Adolf Hitler", and covers his period as a P.O.W.

In 1941 there was a shortage of Heavy Bombers. Aircrew were being trained in Canada. At the time Harry joined there was a small surplus of aircrew so training could take slightly longer and be more thorough. Harry joined the R.A.F. in February 1941 at a recruiting office in Leeds. They sent for him in October 1941 and he was posted to Cardington for his Basic Training.

After a few weeks he was posted to Blackpool where he did a little wireless training plus reading and writing Morse code. In the first week he had to reach a speed of four words a minute. This may not seem much in a world where, today, several million words can be sent electronically each second, but at that time it was a high speed of transmission for a learner, and 15 out of 45 failed the course at this stage and had to cease training.

Harry's next camp was Yatesbury in Wiltshire, where he did more wireless morse code, and started flying in small aircraft for air experience. Next stop was Feltwell and Mildenhall in Norfolk. This was an Operational Squadron flying Wellingtons in 1942.

Following this training, Harry was posted to Cranwell, an Officers College with, annexed to it, No.1 Wireless School, where the serious training started.

A wireless training course maintains a high pace and includes many subjects, including a little navigation and a lot of airmanship. After this it was back to Yatesbury again on a refresher course. Here he had to pass out as a fully fledged Wireless Operator, able to send and receive Morse at 22 words a minute - no mean feat. Then he was on a gunners course, as all wireless operators had to have a second string to their bow. This air gunners training was undertaken at West Freugh and Stranraer, in Scotland, flying two-engined aircraft, "Ansons". This gives rise to the Wop/Ag of which Harry is so proud - Wireless Operator / Air Gunner.

After passing out from gunnery, Harry was posted to an Operation Training Unit at Lossiemouth. Here he received his Sergeant Tapes and individuals were formed into crews.

Harry Ball flew Wellingtons, and was then posted quite near to his home town of Harrogate in Yorkshire - to Marston Moor. An excellent posting. Following this, the next step was a full conversion course at the specialist unit for the Halifax, a four engined bomber. By now it was 1943. After nearly two years of continuous bookwork, training and flying, Harry was posted to his Squadron at last - No. 158 Squadron at Lissett, four miles from Bridlington on the East coast.

The first part of this book describes the period from December 1943 to the day when Harry bailed out over Germany. This is a personal story of life on an Operational Squadron from December 1941 and it covers, in Harry's own words and from his memories, what life was really like. The second part covers the period from becoming a P.O.W. to being released with thousands of other P.O.W.s after an appalling forced march across Germany in the last few weeks of the war. **BLB**

A DANGEROUS GAME

This is my true personal story of life on an Operational Squadron from December 1943, when we arrived on the squadron, until I was released with thousands of other P.O.W.s who were on a forced march in the last few weeks of the war. We were released by Montgomery's Army in 1945.

The first three months of 1944 were cold and windy. We were posted to our conversion unit at Marston Moor in Yorkshire. We had been flying Wellingtons, two-engined bombers. Now we were going to fly Halifax four-engined bombers, so we had a lot of flying to do.

Our crew were ready, willing and able. If we had known to expect at this time that our life expectancy was only a few weeks, I don't think it would have made any difference. The original crew - Pilot, Dutch-Canadian, Van Slyke - Navigator, Canadian, McGillivary - Bomb Aimer, Canadian, MacDonagh - Engineer, Scotsman, Whitelaw - Wireless Air Gunner, English, H Ball - Mid Upper-Gunner, Scotsman, Grant - Rear Gunner, Scotsman, Collingwood - Two spares, Navigator Evans, English and Rear Gunner Mowbury, English.

The four-engined Halifax was continually having new parts fitted, including new and more powerful engines. Even the fin at the back was changed from angular to the square. The trouble was, time was short in those days. It was up to the crews to test all the new equipment. Radar, "G", Mandrill   and Monica were new wireless aids. The last one, Monica, was used to give warning of any approaching aircraft - as the aircraft became closer, it gave off a loud whistling noise, friendly or enemy. We also had to test a new device, "Window", metalic strips designed to fool the enemy. Accidents were happening all the time during training, as well as operations. At Marston Moor we did a lot of flying. All the crews had to be on their toes, but here is one incident to give you an idea of how accidents can happen.

While on take-off and landing from Marston Moor to Snaith, a nearby squadron, three aircraft took off. The first to arrive at Snaith, for some unknown reason, landed in a gun pit. Our pilot made a perfect landing, and was coasting along when the third plane like a giant bird crashed into the back of us. Although there was no loss of life, the Rear Gunner had quite a scare when he saw the whirling blades at each side of his gun turret ripping the tailplane to pieces. He was lucky to escape unhurt. None of the crews came back that night. We stayed overnight, and the next morning a truck took us back to Marston Moor. It was a case of "Three Aircraft Missing".

Although the Halifax was frowned on compared to the Lancaster, a lot of famous people flew in them first, for example, Group Captain Cheshire V.C., Air Vice Marshall Bennett of Pathfinder fame, and Wing Commander Calder. He was one of the first to drop the 22,000lb bomb in a Lancaster. We were both at Lissett 158 Squadron, when he was flying Halifax's.

Now back at Marston Moor, all the crews were hard at it flying day and night if the weather was good. What spare time we had was spent playing cards or visiting the local pub. After a few weeks we were considered to be capable of flying on Operational trips, so we were given a short leave. I took the crew home with me to meet the family at Harrogate. Harrogate was a Receival and Disposal Unit for aircrew fresh from training in Canada - mainly pilots, navigators and bomb-aimers.

In Harrogate, just for a change, everywhere we went were groups of Aircrew! The pubs were packed out. Down at the local pub, The Exchange, the seven of us sat round a table. As it was crowded, it was a bit awkward getting to the bar, so we filled our table with bottled Bass, a dark ale, and we spent the rest of the night there.

My sister Marjorie was dating a London boy who was stationed at Dishforth and was flying Whitlys, two-engined bombers. I think he had already been on several trips. We were posted to 158 Squadron Lissett, four miles from Bridlington on the East coast, and sixty miles from Harrogate, my home town.

The squadron had just received the new Mk3 Halifax and our first job was for the crews to get used to them. We flew many hours day and night, the pilot to get used to the controls, the navigator to plot a course, the bomb-aimer had his bomb-site and practice bombs, the engineer to regulate the flow of petrol to the four engines. My job was to get in touch by Morse Code to as many stations and squadrons as I could and make out a log, which was inspected by the Signals Officer after each trip. The gunners had to fire at Drogues, which were pulled by a smaller plane, also Fighter Affiliation with several planes involved, but most of all we had to work as a team. The new Halifaxes were first used in the 1000 bomber raids of 1944. We even had a mock raid on London when the Germans were quiet.

The life on this squadron was pretty much the same as other camps. Playing cards in the Sergeants Mess, even when they had notices on the walls saying "No Gambling Allowed". No-one took any notice. The food was reasonable in the Mess, but there wasn't much of a variety. We had lots of fruit pies for puddings - Lyons, I think, they were square with fruit inside. With hot custard poured over them, they were delicious. I used to go for seconds. The best card game we used to play was Shoot Pontoon or Blackjack, as the Canadians called it. I was lucky at that game. We had mixed crews, Australians, New Zealanders and South Africans. We made the Mess into quite a gambling den.

Our crew went everywhere together, any spare time we had we spent in Bridlington, which was only four miles - half an hour - away. We were friendly with a group of W.A.A.F.s who were billeted on the Promenade. Most of them worked in the basement of the Pavilion. It was also a dancehall and picture house.

THE ANSON

Going back to Lossiemouth, O.T.U, when we first arrived, all the Aircrew assembled in a large room. It was the responsibility of the pilots to choose their own crews. Five were required for a two-engined Wellington. Later we were posted to our conversion unit, where two more were added, as it needed seven to complete the complement to fly a Halifax bomber.

Later, when I was finally considered as a satisfactory prospect by my eventual pilot, the choice was dramatically limited as the room was nearly empty. I was about five feet two, and looked about sixteen. A Canadian pilot came over to me and said "Would you like to be my wireless operator?" I grabbed the chance and ended up with three Canadians and three Scotsmen. I was the referee!

Later, when we had completed a few trips, Van explained he did not think much of me when he first saw me, but he had no choice - I was the only one left. After our first two trips, when we had all that trouble, he realised I knew my job and had a lot of respect for me. He even started to call me "son". He was a year older then me, big and broad. He acted like a father figure as well as the pilot of a four-engined bomber.

Accidents were happening all the time on the squadron. On two of our trips, we landed without brakes. We crashed through ploughed fields and ditches before coming to a stop. I don't think the powers that be could say anything, as the Wing Commander did the same thing. No-one was hurt - just shaken up. One of our crews had to bail out. Two of the crew had not tightened their harnesses properly and fell through to their deaths. One time, we came in with bombs aboard; they must have got jammed in the bomb bay. It was not unusual for planes to collide when you had one thousand planes in the air, and there is always the risk of bad weather.

My best pal, Leslie Killpatrick, was still training at Lossiemouth, his O.T.U. in Scotland. He was two years younger than I, and was following in my footsteps as I did with my brother, who was two years older. Leslie passed out as a Signaller with an S.Brevy, not as a Wop/AG. How proud we were on leave together, having a drink at the local pub. I mention this now, because he was killed in the same week as I was reported missing believed killed. Both our photos were in the Harrogate papers, Leslie was reported killed in action.

So far I have not mentioned my brother Fred. He joined the R.A.F.
in 1939 and finished two tours in March 1943, as F.L.D.F.C. with
59 trips under his belt. He was also a Wop/AG. I was following in
his footsteps, and now it was my turn. Now that Fred had finished
his tours, our parents were relieved. Now with me it started all
over again.

Our own navigator had to go into hospital with Yellow Jaundice, so
he could not be with us on our first two trips. We had to use a spare
from one of the crews that had split up. His name was Raymond
Lister. I didn't know until 40 years later when I met him at the 158
Club. He survived and was awarded the D.F.C. A lot of aircrew
were stationed at Bridlington training as engineers. They had a
white flash in their caps to say they were under training.

On the 20th of January, 1944, the great day had arrived. Although
we did a lot of training up until this time, the squadron was still
operational, and raids to different targets took place.

We were taking it easy in the mess when an officer walked in and
said "Ops tonight lads". If you asked me at that moment how I felt
hearing those words, maybe if I had been a better writer I could
have told you. After two years' training I was keen to have a go.

Later, each of the crews went to his own section, and then on to the
briefing room. The room was full of aircrew waiting for instructions
about the target.

The target was the big city, Berlin. After getting all the
information and collecting our parachutes, we proceeded to the
assembly line, where trucks were waiting to take us to our aircraft.
This night we were flying "E" for Eric.

When I wrote my last book, "Two Brothers at War", some people
said it should have been bigger, and it could do with a bit more
embroidery, so here goes.

Although the ground staff were very busy, and all the rest of the
crews preparing to take off in their different aircraft, inwardly

everyone seemed quiet. The well-trained crews got on with their jobs without any fuss. How different they were to the American aircrews - certainly more reserved. Little did I know I would be with the Americans in a P.O.W. camp in East Prussia, in a few weeks' time.

When we climbed into our aircraft, although the ground staff had tested all the equipment, we did it again. Our spare navigator was Raymond Lister. In my little space in the aircraft, I was separated from the rest of the crew. I had to use the intercom to get orders and so on. On the right of me was a curtain which separated me from the pilot, navigator, engineer and bomb-aimer. The two gunners were in their turrets, testing their guns.

I was feeling nervous on take-off, thinking what would happen if we crashed with our load of bombs on board. When I was at Feltwell, in Norfolk, during my wireless training, I saw a Wellington take off fully loaded with bombs, then nose-dive into the ground. There was a huge explosion and all the crew were killed. I went to the funeral at Mildenhall, a few miles away.As soon as we were on our way and over the sea, the gunners fired their guns to see if they were ready for action. On my left side was a small window, which was covered most of the time because of the blackout. Every so often I took a peep out to see what was going on. We took off with the rest of the crews at about 8 o'clock at night, in the dark. I was not scared, yet at the same time we were going into the unknown.

I just got on with my job, and didn't think about it. People would say how brave we were, but I don't think that came into it, certainly not at the time. (I felt proud though.) Everything went well for about an hour, then we started having trouble with two of the engines. We had no choice but to drop our bombs into the sea and return to base. It would have been suicide to have carried on to the target. Three crews had to return because of trouble of some sort. One of 158's Halifaxes failed to return. They were shot down near Hamburg, and all the crew were killed. On this raid the R.A.F. lost 35 aircraft. We were very disappointed on having to return, although it happens to most crews at some time or another. You always get the feeling people might think you got scared, and made an excuse to abort the trip. I was alone in my little alcove, feeling very sorry for myself.

They used to say if you could survive four or five trips, you had a good chance of finishing your tour. (Who were they kidding?) I read a book on statistics that said that on Halifax squadrons the chances of finishing a tour was between 2% and 8%. That was more like it.

After missing all the excitement over Berlin, we had our egg and chips and went back to the old Nisson hut.

In the mess the next day, we heard the news of the Berlin raid, and then once again that familiar voice, "Ops tonight". Back to the briefing. It was the 21st of January, 1944, and the target was Magdeburg, about 80 kms from Berlin. It was the first major raid on this target. All the way to the target enemy fighters had got into the bomber stream and a lot of combats took place. 158 lost one plane. 50 planes were lost to the squadrons. When we were over the target, I had a look out of my side window. Plenty of flak flying about, and the ground itself was a mass of flames. So far it seemed to be an easy trip. Because of high winds we were slightly off course, and when we were nearly home, the pilot realised we might not have enough petrol to get back to base. There was no panic when the pilot asked me to send out an S.O.S.

I have not told you about our journey to the target. One of our Wireless Aids was Window, metallic strips which were packed together in bundles, and as we passed the enemy coast, I threw it down a small chute at the side of me. As the slipstream caught it, it burst into hundreds of pieces. This interfered with the German long range frequency direction finders. The Germans had almost the same equipment as we had. When we had almost reached the target we had a message from Group, giving us a frequency. This was a short range frequency which the German night fighters used. We had to jam it with our Morse keys. In between we had to listen out on our Marconi sets, in case a message came in from Base.

After a short time, and I had been in touch with Base, the pilot asked me to get a Q.D.M., a special Q code which is a course to steer to get back to Base. From then on, things began to move quickly as the plane was going down. We were probably about 1500 feet at this time. The engines started to cut, and the engineers had to control the petrol going to the engines. It was then that the pilot gave orders to get ready to ditch into the sea. As the Q.D.M. was third class, I was asked to try again. This time I managed to get a second-class bearing.

Now as the bomb-aimer, who was flat on his face in the nose of the aircraft, saw waves below him he notified the pilot we were close to the coastline. In the meantime, while the crew were dodging about, the pilot gave orders to bail out. We had a different spare navigator with us on this trip, Evans. Our own navigator was still in hospital. He reported to the pilot that his radar wasn't working.

All the time we were slowly losing height. I took off my headset and, with great difficulty, put on my parachute which was strapped at the side of me, then went straight to the rear of the aircraft where the escape hatch was already open.

On arriving, the rear gunner, Collingwood, and navigator Evans were sitting on the edge of the escape hatch. I don't know what they were waiting for. Maybe they hadn't heard the pilot give the order to bail out, and thought we were still ditching. Anyway, we will never know. I rolled out between them, pulling the ripcord on my parachute, and hit the ground straight away. The night was dark and I had no idea where I had landed. I hit a hedge and landed in a ploughed field, seconds between life and death.

The Q.D.M.s I obtained for the pilot must have been dead on, for I landed near the outer perimeter of the airfield. Poor Collingwood and Evans both hit the ground before their chutes opened. What a way to go. Collingwood was only 18. I must have been the last to leave the aircraft - that is, alive, at about 500 feet. We were told it was suicide to jump out below 1000 feet. The pilot stayed in the aircraft, and the bomb-aimer wouldn't leave him. They crash-landed and escaped unhurt, on the edge of the squadron. McDonagh found the bodies of the two crew. They lay on the ground as if asleep, with their unopened chutes beside them, bleeding from their nose, eyes and ears. Years later when I saw McDonagh in Canada, he said there was only a pint of petrol left in the tanks of the plane (or so the ground staff had told him).

There was no panic with the crew, we did what we were trained to do automatically.

Back to the bailing out. After picking up my parachute I walked back to camp. Quite a crowd was waiting outside, including my Signals Leader, Sandy Sandall. He ended up as a Squadron Leader, D.F.C. and Bar. His first words were well done, good show, or words to that effect. He said all the section had been praying for us. They knew we were near, but could not see us, even though they had fired a Very Pistol and Rockets. We never saw them - it was too dark.

Now I would become a member of the Caterpillar Club, and I would receive a Gold Caterpillar with red eyes, and, engraved on the back, Sgt. H. Ball, for having my life saved by parachute. I remember waiting in a small room to be debriefed, and was thinking about all sorts of things. After all, up until this time I had no idea what had happened to the rest of the crew. Three of us managed to bail out without injury, two stayed in the aircraft and landed without injury when the plane crashed, and two were killed when their chutes didn't open. I felt numb with shock. So this was our Baptism of Fire.

After this episode, the crew were given two weeks Survival Leave, which was the usual thing when there was loss of life. When our W.A.A.F. friends in Bridlington heard the news about Collingwood, there were a lot of tears flowing. He was well liked and was going out with one of them. We got on well with the W.A.A.F.s and spent a lot of time with them in their billet on the Promenade. Our engineer, Whitelaw, was a smashing pianist, so everywhere we went, if a piano was available, we drew a crowd, whether it was in the mess, W.A.A.F. billet or in a pub, we had a good sing-song. My favourite was Boogy Woogy and Stagecoach played together. In the W.A.A.F.s billet we had to be out by 10 o'clock, but when the Orderly Sergeant came round with her torch, she would shine it at us and say, "Oh, Van Slyke's crew here again" and then walk out.

When we first arrived on the squadron, we went straight to the Sgts mess, and in the main room, a group of aircrew were having a discussion about a photo in a newspaper. When we found out what it was about, we got a surprise. Apparently, a Rear Gunner had been shining a torch out of his turret when he was on ops, to attract German fighters. His picture was in the paper. As far as I can remember, he may have shot one or two planes down. It was hardly fair on the rest of the crew. Our job was to avoid enemy action, drop our bombs on the target and get out as soon as possible. About a year ago I got this story confirmed by a Mr Motterhead, who is in charge of the 158 Club. He said the gunner was posted to another squadron, but he didn't last very long. It takes all sorts.

Many crews were asked to volunteer to fly on ops when they were trying to get numbers together for the 1000 bomber raids. It is still a mystery what happened to my pal Leslie. He could have been one of those crews. The only news I had was from his sister, that his plane took off from Lossiemouth, O.T.U., and nose-dived into the bay. Their bodies were never found. I have no proof of this, but these sorts of accidents did happen. When on leave and I was around, Leslie always stayed at our house, even though he had a gran in the next street, and a mother living in Thirsk, twenty-two miles away. We were more like brothers.

Before going on ops again, when the weather was bad, most of the crews were sent on a Battle Course to Driffield, with the army. We were all dressed in denims with our rank covered up. We had to take orders from the army.

It was quite an experience, blacking our faces and raiding a mock machine-gun post, at night in the pouring rain. We also did unarmed combat, gunnery and route marches, etc. If I remember rightly, the Skipper and I were caught cycling without lights, and were fined ten shillings each at Driffield.

After about a week, we returned to the squadron feeling fresh to go on Ops. After our experience at Magdeburg, and we were on leave in Harrogate, I went to the pictures, The Central Cinema. To my surprise on the Pathe Gazette News was a picture of a target over Germany. Big 1000 bomber raid on Magdeburg, and before my eyes was a picture of the target on fire, exactly as I had seen it over the target. I don't know what happened to me, but I fell asleep in the cinema. I have never done that before. The shock must have affected me more than I realised.

Van Slyke and McGillivary stayed at our house for a few days, then went elsewhere. McDonagh went down to London by himself. Whitelaw and Grant went home to Scotland. Once back on the squadron, we started flying again, mostly training. Then we heard that our crew was going to be split up, as they usually did when there was loss of life, but instead of making us unsettled, it bound us together, so McDonagh and I went to see the Commanding Officer, and told him that if they split us up, we wouldn't fly again. His answer was, seeing that you seem keen to keep together, it is alright by me. This was a court marshall offence, if the officer wanted to charge us. You see, when crews first get together, you take a chance they are capable of doing their jobs properly. The best way to find out is in action.

In the sergeants mess, we were talking when a sergeant walked in and I recognised him straight away. It was Louie Craven. We attended the same school and were born in the same street in Harrogate. That night, Ops were on and his crew took part. When he did not return, we thought he had been killed or taken prisoner. I did not know the truth until 44 years later. I met his sister in Harrogate, and she explained that his squadron was at Driffield, and sometimes they went to Lissett and took off from there. A few days later, I am sad to say, he was killed at Nuremburg when 90 planes were lost. I never saw much action, such as going through a flak barrage, or spotting and occasional German fighter trying to catch us unaware. I just did my usual job.

Once you start on Ops, if you are lucky you can get through them pretty quickly, sometimes flying on two or three on consecutive nights. Between trips, we spent most of our spare time with the W.A.A.F.s. They were good company, and kept our minds off things.

Ops again, this time Augsburg, and our target was almost completely destroyed by high explosive and fires. 158 had no losses, but the other squadrons lost 21 planes. Grant, one of our gunners, had a chunk of perspex knocked out of his turret or dome. It must have been a near miss, as he could only find one hole.

Planes my brother flew in were hit many times. He flew on Ops in Wellingtons, Hampdens and Lancasters. Luck was always with him. Imagine 59 trips!

On the 1st of March 1944, we flew in H for Harry, and our target was Stuttgart. We did about two and a half hours flying and then had to return. Engine trouble again. 158 lost no planes, because the German night fighters could not make contact due to the heavy clouds. Our Wing Commander always kept us busy when there were no Ops on. We did quite a few local flights and plenty of training. On one flight, when two pilots flew together on Fighter Affiliation, Van Slyke was the main pilot and had to dodge about a bit. He made the other pilot very sick. The gunners had to be alert all the time, as they were our only protection. The more practice they had, the better it was for us.

One bit of news came from out of the blue from McDonagh, the bomb aimer. When the rest of the crew were on leave, McDonagh volunteered to do more trips with another crew. The two targets were tough - Leipzig and Stuttgart. To him it was something to do to pass the time until we came back off leave. He had gone to London, spent his money and then come back to camp broke while he was still on leave, after refusing to fly if they split us up, and then going solo himself.

On March the 6th, 1944, we went to Trappes in France. This was a good raid, with no losses on the squadrons. No German fighters were sighted.

March the 7th, 1944, we went to Le Mans in France, with no losses to the squadrons.

March the 13th, 1944, we went to Le Mans again, just to make sure. The same again, no fighters about. But 158 lost one plane.

When I was a P.O.W. in East Prussia, I remember an aircrew chap saying he was the only survivor on that raid. All the rest of his crew had been killed, and he wasn't very pleased about it, it being such an easy target. Although I am explaining about the targets we were on, smaller raids were taking place at the same time all over Europe.

Now changing the subject, when you are getting old your memory gets a bit vague, but still there are happenings you can never forget. On the lighter side, I will tell you three stories.

First, the room we slept in was a Nisson hut. We had a stove in the centre of the room. I cannot remember what fuel we had, all I know is that it was always cold. McDonagh had the right idea. He had a full length inner flying suit , where he got it from I don't know. He used to wear it in bed. It was funny to see him sitting up in bed reading a book. It was made of fur fabric. He looked like a huge teddy bear.

The next two episodes happened in the same place, The Pavilion, Bridlington. Our crew had been in the dancehall, and it was about 10 o'clock at night, and we wanted to get back to camp early. I was walking up the centre aisle when an airman put his elbow in front of me and to my surprise he said to me "Who are you pushing?" He grabbed the lapels of my battledress. Collingwood, who was stood next to me, almost straight away grabbed hold of the airman and said "What did you say?" The airman went away meekly. He'd probably had too much to drink.

One night when it was very late, too late to get back to camp, the W.A.A.F.s we were with suggested sleeping between the seats of the cinema, though I think they were kidding us. However we did. Next morning the W.A.A.F.s woke us up and asked what we would like for breakfast. It was about 6 o'clock in the morning. The basement was the cookhouse. Rows of trays were laid out for the airmen's breakfast. We saw mostly bacon. They told us to help ourselves. (P.S. The crew slept by themselves.)

At this moment, things were going well for us. One night we had sometime off, and the crew were together. We stopped at one of the local pubs for a drink. We were sat around one table deep in conversation, when an R.A.F. officer came over to us (he had been sitting at the next table). He said "Are you Van Slyke's crew?" We replied "Yes". "Well, I am your adjutant. We have been hearing a lot about you and the bad luck you have experienced. You are the talk of the squadron. We think that, as you have survived a few trips and are settling down, you will be able to complete your tour." Little did he know that a week later we would be shot down over Berlin, with three of the crew killed and four taken prisoner. The previous three trips were uneventful as far as we were concerned.

On March the 15th, 1944, we bombed Stuttgart again, and just before we reached the target, the German fighters arrived and fierce combats ensued. We were lucky again; no losses to 158. But the other squadrons lost 30 aircraft to fighters.

A bit of a mystery happened on one of our trips, when a message came through from Group. It consisted of code in groups of five, forming a block of about twenty-five. I received most of the message, just missed two or three letters. When decoded, the message seemed to be: Enemy fighters on your track, take evasive action, and a map reading was given. I know very few of the wireless operators received the message fully, and no-one seemed to have any information about it. On enquiring, they said it must have been a hoax to keep the w/ops alert.

On March the 18th, we flew to Frankfurt in force - 846 planes took part and much damage was done. 158 lost one plane by fighter.

On March the 22nd we went to Frankfurt again. This time we had a scare. Frankfurt was noted for its searchlights, and we were surrounded by them trying to pick us out. Suddenly they moved to one side, forming a pathway. We flew on regardless, expecting fighters to be waiting at the other end. Luck was with us. Finally we returned safely to Base. We must have had a guardian angel that night. 158 lost two aircraft by fighters, and the other squadrons lost thirty-three aircraft. The Americans had been there on several daylight raids and the place was a pile of rubble. I know for sure, having walked through the town when taken prisoner.

And our last trip was March the 24th, 1944, the date of our ill-fated trip to Berlin. This was the last time I saw England for 14 months. Out of 811 aircraft, 73 were lost. 158 lost two aircraft - one was ours. Very high winds were encountered on the way to the target, and many planes were blown off course. The Flak Batteries were believed to have shot down fifty planes, and fourteen others by fighters on the run in to the target, including ours. The other crew 158 lost was flown by Pilot Officer Simpson. He sent a message to base that he was having severe engine trouble and would have to return. Nothing was heard from him, until a message came through stating that one of our squadron aircraft had crashed on the shoreline in Norfolk. The pilot tried to force land, but struck a sea mine setting off a tremendous explosion, and killed everyone on board. A few days earlier, we had been playing cards with the crew.

We were attacked by a Junkers 88, the new version which fired Cannon shells from the nose of the aircraft. In most of our bombers, we had no protection underneath, unlike the American planes. The Germans were quick to notice this and were having a field day, at our expense. The Germans used to come up from underneath and blow us to pieces. When on our run in to target to drop our bombs, the bomb aimer lay flat in the nose of the aircraft, ready to use his bomb sight. When the German fighter came in from underneath, McDonagh got the full burst of the Cannon shells down his right side, leg and ankle, also setting two engines on fire.

Years later, when I saw him in Canada, he said he didn't feel the first burst much, but when the fighter came in again and gave him another burst down his side, he said it did sting a bit. Joking aside, by this time he was in a bad way.

Halifax "S" went into a dive. I heard the pilot shout "For Christ sake get out of this aircraft." At the same time I heard the rear gunner screaming "I can't get out of my turret." From where I was in the front of the aircraft, it was impossible for me to help him. When we were first attacked, I was busy on my radio set, and to some extent isolated from the rest of the crew. Only through the intercom could I hear what was going on. Then thud, thud, thud, and I could feel the cannon shells hitting the aircraft as it lurched to one side. The curtain at the side of me blew in, and I could see the nose was on fire. Blood was running down the forehead of the navigator. Fortunately it was only a scratch. At this point I did not know the bomb aimer was badly wounded.

I saw the front hatch was open, and he was going through. By now the plane was out of control, and in a spin. I tried to put on my parachute, which was at the side of me, but as soon as it was released, it went straight to the roof, taking all my strength to pull it down and fix it to my harness. At this time the plane was rolling all over the place, completely out of control. Struggling to the escape hatch, I managed to roll out into the slipstream. It was quite understandable how crews got trapped in a plane, as it was going almost straight down. It is an experience I wouldn't wish on anyone.

Fires were burning down below, like one big carpet, with the explosions of the bombs and stricken aircraft going down. 73 that night. It was quite a sight.

What worried me was landing right in the middle of it. As luck would have it, I drifted away from the target area until it was completely black. Before I went into the blackness, I saw, silhoutted against the skyline, a dome similar to St. Pauls Cathedral back in England. Weeks later, published by a German magazine in the prison camp, appeared the same picture.

I landed somewhere in a dyke near the Brandenburg Gate. I calculated we had been flying at about 20,000 feet.

As this part of the story is about the squadron, I won't go into any P.O.W. life, except for one little story. One of our pilots from 158 Squadron, Sgt Hughes, was shot down over Nuremburg a week later. 90 planes were lost that night. We more or less travelled together from Frankfurt in Germany through Poland, to Stalagluft 6 in East Prussia. We were in the same hut in the camp and, except when he left the column on the forced march at the end of the war, we were together most of the time.

Sgt Hughes was captured with another 158 chap, Killagrew, an engineer. The reason I am telling this story is that his brother had put an advert in the R.A.F.A. Magazine, asking anyone that knew him to get in touch. One of three brothers, all pilots, was writing a book. Stephen Hughes had been killed in a plane accident in 1948, and he had no way of knowing what sort of story his brother had to tell.

I helped him with limited information. When I first met these two 158 chaps in the camp, they told me that our squadron had almost been wiped out.

It would have been interesting to have been in the W.A.A.F.s billet when they heard the news that we had been reported missing. We were more, like a family group. It is the families back home which suffer the most. My brother Fred married his Lincoln fiance on the 24th of March, 1943. He went home on his wedding anniversary (the date I failed to return) to see Mother. On arrival, she looked very upset, and he asked our sister Marjorie why. She said "Harry didn't return from operations last night." Mother recievd the usual telegram but it was three months later, in June, before she knew I was alive and a prisoner in German hands.

There are so many things we can imagine might have been the reason the three crew were unable to get out of the aircraft, apart from the obvious - the plane had been in a dive. The pilot could have been badly wounded, as he was in the nose of the aircraft when it sustained all the fire. He could have heard the rear gunner screaming "I can't get out of my turret" and stayed in the aircraft in an attempt to control the plane and so give the crew a better chance of getting out.

On our second trip, Magdeburg, why were Collingwood and Evans waiting near the escape hatch, instead of jumping before me? These things will never be known.

This is the end of the first part of my true story on the life of one crew on an Operational Squadron.

JU 88
Drawing by Harry Ball

HARRY BALL
Under training
in 1941

BLACKPOOL, 1941. Aircrew Training
Harry Ball is on the third row down five in from the right.

WEST FREUGH, SCOTLAND.
Harry Ball is on a gunnery course, and stands on his own at the
right hand side. Taken after a hard night out on the town!

HARRY BALL,
promoted to Sergeant

LESLIE - my best pal,
killrd the week I was shot down

Bomb aimer   Rear Gunner   Navigator
McDonagh   Collingwood   McGillivary

"For you, the War is over . . . !"

AN UNWILLING GUEST

March the 24th was an unfortunate day for us, also 50 officers from Sargan, who were escaping at the time. They were caught and shot by the S.S. It is my hope that in writing this book, that it will be possible to give readers an insight into the life of a Prisoner Of War, when incarcerated as "Unwilling Guests" of Adolf Hitler.

With the help of a few sketches, drawn by others, mainly fellow prisoners at Heydekrug, in East Prussia, Thorn in Poland and Fallingbostol in Germany, an overall picture is produced.

Some of the pictures appeared in a book, "Handle With Care", by authors R. Anderson and D. Westmacott; both ex-prisoners themselves, and I have no wish to take credit for the work of others. Having been a prisoner in all three camps, I considered it an appropriate opportunity to add a few lines of my personal experiences.

At the age of 72 years, my memory is not as clear as it used to be. However, many things are so deeply rooted, they can never be completely forgotten.

On the few operations our crew managed to complete, we had more than our share of bad luck. Having bailed out from roughly 20,000 feet, with freezing level about 1,000 feet, naturally it was very cold, especially as my gloves were left in the aircraft in the obvious emergency of leaving the plane, as it could have exploded at any moment. Sensibly, I put my hand inside my tunic and the other inside the zip of my trousers. Frostbite was a strong possibility. It seemed a lifetime before landing.

Having landed in a dyke, in March winds, I was pulled along at high speed. I eventually released myself, removed the harness and buried it with the chute, etc, under the side of the bank, as told during training. Being saturated and cold and, to be honest, without a clue where I was, having been working on my wireless set when attacked, later I learnt what really happened. On the ground, anti-aircraft guns were blazing away and the noise of the aircraft heading for home in the distance was considerable.

Suddenly my mind was in a whirl, however. Finding a safe place to hide was uppermost in my thoughts. It was close to midnight on the 24th of March 1944. All around were woodlands. I kept walking as if in a dream. Coming to a farm with a few outbuildings, I selected the largest and attempted to climb into the loft. It was difficult, as I couldn't find a ladder, only 12-inch square posts, and it was almost impossible to manage, being cold and wet through. Luckily it was stacked with straw, which made a comfortable bed. My thoughts were running wild. Where was I? How had the rest of the crew fared? Had any of them been wounded? Did they all vacate the aircraft safely?

After a while, sleep overcame me and I was oblivious to my ordeal for a short time. On waking up, it was light and the sun was shining through a hole in the roof. Feeling a bit uncomfortable, I removed my flying boots and laid them on the straw to dry out. A short time later, hearing noises and the sound of German voices, I put my flying boots on and before I could stand up, a German soldier came over to me, carrying a hefty stick and threatening me with it. Suddenly he pointed to a whistle on my battledress I carried in case of ditching in the sea. Taking it off, I gave it to him and that had a calming effect. He pointed to a ladder at the side of the loft, which I missed the night before. He beckoned me to climb down, and, at the edge, I had the fright of my life. Approximately thirty men and women, all carrying farm implements of some sort, were below. In the mood they were in, they could have cut me to pieces. They probably felt sorry for me. Although 22 years old at the time, I looked about 16. The Germans called us "Terror Fliegers" and "Luft Gangsters". At this time I was a threat to no-one. Later, it was explained I had been at the Brandenburg Estate Farm, and the barn I had chosen was the meeting place for the farm workers in the district.

I was marched off to the local jail with a crowd of people in attendance. This was my first introduction to a prison when I was placed in a cell.

As the Germans said, "For you, the war is over." After about an hour, they came into my cell with a German sausage. Partly raw meat, and some blackish bread, it was quite a time before I had the courage to eat it.

As the weeks rolled on in the prison camps, we were glad to eat anything. The cell was small, with only a little peep hole in the door, where the guards periodically spied on me. After all, I was a dangerous prisoner (ha ha!)

The next morning, they gave me a cup of coffee made out of acorns (or so I was told). Subsequently, they put me into a private vehicle. The Germans wore trenchcoats. I had no idea whether they were Police or Gestapo. Our destination was Berlin, and on arrival we parked outside a high building with Swasticas and eagles in abundance. German soldiers were everywhere. I guess it was similar to our Air Ministry. Next stop was a large room, with male and female officers behind desks. most of the Germans seemed to know a little English, and they told me to strip to my vest and pants, most likely looking for combs and studs intended to be used as compasses. I was rather embarrassed, everyone using me for a peep show.

Dressing myself, I was then taken back to the car and driven to a Berlin railway station. I met my navigator there, the only officer in the crew. Strangely, the station did not appear to be damaged by the air raids.

It was an electric train. We stood all the way to Frankfurt. Luckily we were guarded by Luftwaffe troops with guns drawn. We would not have an earthly chance to escape. The Germans just stared and meant business. Looking through the carriage window, whilst waiting in the station, I saw German soldiers giving the Nazi salute to their officers. Over the public address system in the station came the voice of a woman shouting "Achtung Achtung" (Attention). It seemed strange, only a few days previously, I was in Bridlington on the Yorkshire coast, and now I was in the heart of Germany.

After travelling for many hours, we arrived at Frankfurt. The navigator and myself had to walk through the centre of the city, which was a mass of rubble, hardly a building left standing. Once again we were escorted by Luftwaffe guards, this time the locals were in a bad mood, shaking their fists at us and shouting. Could they be blamed? Very likely they had lost friends and family during the bombing. We had been on two night operations to Frankfurt, and the Americans had been on several daylight raids also. To the

Germans we were still Terror Fliegers and Luft Gangsters, not taking into consideration the German raids on London and other cities.

We walked to the Interrogation Centre and were placed in separate cells, small rooms with windows, shutters and bars. There was a radiator in the room, though it wasn't needed, it was stifling. Probably the Germans did it intentionally, to lower our resistance for the interrogation to follow.

There was the usual aperture in the door where the guards checked to see if we were okay. If you wanted to go to the lavatory the guard was called, who escorted us. On one of these occasions, I had a glimpse of my mid-upper-gunner, Grant. We had a few words. He told me he had managed to bail out but was slightly burnt on the neck. He was lucky; he did not know what had happened to the rest of the crew.

Later on in the prison camp at Heydekrug, in East Prussia, we managed to get the news through. I don't know the details, but four managed to bail out. The remaining three crew members were trapped in the aircraft when it crashed to earth.

The navigator, mid-upper-gunner and myself, wireless operator, successfully bailed out. The navigator was hit on the forehead, though only superficially, fortunately. As he was in the nose of the aircraft, the bomb aimer, McDonagh, suffered seriously as he was laid flat attending to his bomb sight, in preparation for the run in to the target. When the Junkers 88 came in from underneath, he got the worst of it. When McDonagh arrived at the prison camp three weeks after us, he was still wearing his flying boots. The right one was covered in blood and cut to ribbons. He said he was keeping the boot as a souvenir.

The rest of the crew gave me all the news. When McDonagh bailed out, he was in a shocking state, and when the navigator found him he was delirious, saying a German soldier had struck him with a rifle butt. There was no alternative but to stay with him, so he forfeited his own opportunity to escape. Crews are duty bound to support each other in trouble.

Next morning the Germans picked him up. He was taken to hospital in Berlin, where he was treated surprisingly well under the circumstances. Under doctor's orders he was given chicken soup and other nourishing food. His weight dropped from eleven stones to six stones. The surgeon informed him that 48 pieces of metal were removed from his body.

The remainder of the crew were trapped in the aircraft, unable to escape. The details were not known until later.

The pilot, Van Slyke, engineer Whitelaw and a spare rear gunner, Mowbray, were all killed. The aircraft plunged to earth at Pausin, 25 kilometres north of Potsdam. Among the twisted remains were the bodies of the rest of the crew.

The day following my arrival at Frankfurt, I was escorted by a guard to see the Interrogation Officer. He met me at the door and was unexpectedly polite, saying "Would you like a cigarette?" I replied "I don't smoke."

Sitting down, he then offered me a biscuit, which I accepted gratefully. He then said "I want you to answer a few questions, though most of the information is already known - I just want confirmation."

My reply was, "I can only give you my number, rank and name." He wanted to know the obvious, such as the squadron I came from, and where it was situated. During our training we were warned to expect this reception.

The officer continued to ask the same question and I couldn't avoid smiling, after repeating the same answer every time. This annoyed him, and he warned me I could be taken out and shot, saying "You are not wearing your identity disc. You could be a spy." Naturally he was right. I had left them in the billet. However I was returned to my cell for future interrogation.

Our food consisted of black bread and thin soup. Heaven alone knows what it consisted of, and German coffee. This was the worst to accept, and I was perpetually hungry.

Each bed had a straw mattress and one blanket. This was never needed, as the radiator was on permanently. I now have first-hand knowledge of how animals live in cages, constantly walking up and down in a confined area. The room was approximately six feet by twelve feet. To get some exercise, I walked up and down the room until I was tired. Fortunately I didn't smoke, and didn't pine for a cigarette all the time, as some poor souls did.

The voices of American aircrew could be heard passing through. Strangely, the interrogators didn't seem to think they were very important so far as extracting information was concerned, and were only held for a couple of days. We were there for twelve days. On the last day, the officer asked me the same questions. Again I gave the same answers. He then left the room, leaving some papers on the table (intentionally, of course). These I read upside down, and on the front page was "A Flight 158 Lissett" clearly seen, which was correct. He still did not get confirmation from me. When he came into the room again, he said "You are going to see some of your mates in a Prisoner of War camp. For you the war is over."

After the war, I saw my navigator, McGillivary, in London, and later in Canada. He said he had divulged the information after giving the rest of the crew a chance to escape. It was no secret anyway; the Germans were efficient in extracting information from all sources. From the centre of Berlin we arrived at our destination.

Quite a crowd had accumulated - P.O.W.s, mostly Allied aircrew. German fighters had obviously been busy claiming their quota of victories. We were ordered into cattle trucks. Each one had three compartments, roughly twenty men each side with the German guards in between. We had to survive there for five days and nights. In the centre of our compartment was a trough intended as a lavatory. "Too embarrassing". Periodically the train stopped so the opportunity was taken to see to the needs of nature. Space was at a premium. We crouched together like sardines. The only light was a slit in the side of the truck which was quite high up. It was a problem to distinguish night from day when the doors were closed.

One night I woke up with someone stretched across my lower limbs. I was numb from the waist down and feeling claustrophobic.

It took all my self control to stop screaming. Most nights, we were shunted into railway sidings to try to avoid the Allied bombing. Several P.O.W.s were killed when the trucks were attacked.

On one occasion, when stopping at a railway station, I can't remember where, a German Red Cross nurse came over to speak to one of our airmen. He knew a little German. She pointed at me and inquired how old I was, being slightly built and looking to be about 16 years old. Actually I was 22. Those five days were dreadful. We travelled out of Germany through Poland and into East Prussia to Stalag 6. We saw little of the scenery throughout. It appeared to be mostly woodland. However, we saw very little from the truck. It makes one wonder how many Jews and political prisoners had travelled in these trucks and then onto the gas chambers.

Whilst travelling through Germany and Poland, we had only been a few miles from the Death Camps. Until the end of the war it had been a well-kept secret. On our journey, the Germans gave us soup, bread and coffee. We were hungry all the time, having barely enough to keep us alive. At the commencement of the war, all prisoners passing through Frankfurt were given an attache case containing one food parcel, a razor, soap, toothbrush and most of the usual necessities. However, when we arrived at our destination, no Red Cross parcels or anything else were forthcoming. They did not appear to exist.

Arriving at our destination, we were marched to the camp, and on approaching the main compound, the P.O.W.s were waiting to greet us. A voice from the crowd shouted "Hello Bally", and to my surprise it was Taffy Gibbs. We last met in Blackpool in 1941. He failed his wireless course, and then trained as an air gunner. He was shot down a few weeks before me. Being a comical chap, he wore a badge on his tunic - "The champion beer drinker of Wales". Grant was already in camp. McDonagh arrived three weeks later. Heydekrug at this time held 3000 British P.O.W.s and a similar number of Americans, all aircrew. Initially we were placed in tents containing three-tier bunks - uncomfortable, but adequate. A little extra food we had was scrounged from outside the cookhouse, mostly vegetable peelings. We at our food off a long table in the tent. It was April now and still very cold. One would think the entire R.A.F. were here. All aircrew categories were present. They had flown in Hampdens, Blenheims, Whitleys, Sterlings, Wellingtons, Halifaxes and Lancasters, and many other aircraft. The first two airmen shot down in 1939 were in our camp, namely Slattery and Booth. Regrettably, both are no longer with us. After several weeks we were transferred and upgraded to the American huts, approximately 70 men to a hut.

I had a bottom bunk, and almost straight away two Americans asked if they could start digging a tunnel under my bed. Obviously I agreed, reasoning that the Germans would not think escaping operations would not commence so soon. They dug down six feet, and about six feet across. Next morning, it was all flooded. One of the Americans was tall, the other small and fat. His nickname was The Mole.

Stalag 6 comprised of four brick barracks, each divided into nine rooms. There were a dozen or so wooden huts, two cookhouses and two latrines. It was a large camp surrounded by woodlands and split into compounds. Outside the camp was a wire fence inside a small fence, about two feet high. Attached to these at intervals were boards with a message - "Anyone going beyond this fence will be shot without warning". On each corner of the compound was a Poston Box or Machine Gun Post. Anyone trying to escape would be covered from all angles. Outside the compound, to make sure, were German guard dogs, therefore the odds of successfully completing an escape by jumping over the wire were nil. In the tents we did a lot of card playing. McDonagh came to see me most days, as well as Grant. Cigarettes substituted for money in the camp. Mostly I was lucky. Just before we were released, McDonagh owed me 500 cigarettes. Not taken seriously of course. Later, when I visited him in Canada, he couldn't remember it!

The Red Cross were supposed to issue one parcel per week to each man. One period of ten weeks we had none at all, and in between, we had to manage on German food and bartering. The situation was so bad that at one stage we had one parcel to share between seven men. The rest were German rations. Imagine sharing a tin of condensed milk - about two spoonfuls each.

My mother arranged with the Red Cross to send me one parcel a week. Actually I received one in fourteen months. Mother gave money to the Red Cross. As I understand it, letters and parcels went to Sargan 3 and were then distributed to all the other camps. It was amazing how the mail could get through from Canada, Australia and America more quickly than from the U.K. When the word was heard that mail was in it was very exciting, though often disappointing for many due to the delay.

Tunnels were built at Heydekrug, and some escaped. Many were caught again, and put in the cooler or cells. Whilst I was there, I had no knowledge of the work in the tunnels. It was arranged by the escape committee in strict secrecy. The Germans took away some of our bed boards so they could not be used to shore up the tunnels.

Our camp leader, Dixie Dean, was shot down on the 10th of September, 1940. He was a pilot on Whitleys. Quite a few Australians were P.O.W.s and they were keen on cricket and football, and also American baseball. They managed to get all the equipment to play.The Germans issued a few cigarettes, but most of them came from the Canadian and American food parcels usually containing 200 cigarettes, so one can understand it was mostly the Canadians and Americans who ran the camp shops.

One of our spare time occupations was walking round the compound, usually in groups, talking and shooting the line. Food parcels, when they came, contained a variety of things such as thick round biscuits which were soaked overnight in milk. The next day, they were double the size. The milk was powdered and in tins called Klim, "milk" reversed. We had a small stove to do a little cooking. A group of us clubbed together and supplied ingredients to make a cake, such as broken biscuits, bread, cake and so on. It worked, though it was depressed in the middle and weighed a ton, but it was still edible.

The Yanks tried a variety of things, for instance passing through our camp was a stream with frogs in it. They tried eating the frogs, even grass and small bulb-like plants. When first arriving at the huts, we met two 158 Squadron aircrew, Hughs, pilot, and Killagrew, flight engineer. They were shot down a week after our crew. They gave us some dreadful news about our squadron almost being wiped out over the last few weeks.

Nurnburg was attacked on the 30th of March, 1944. 90 planes and 600 aircrew were lost, more than likely two thirds of them killed, the rest wounded and taken prisoner. No wonder my second book is called "A Dangerous Game".

Although not allowed to work officially, occasionally men from each hut were allowed out in turn with a wheelbarrow to collect fuel, wooden stumps left when the trees were cut down. A prisoner invented a "blower" which we took outside to do our cooking, make drinks and so on. It consisted of a wheel inside a case which spun round by turning a handle at the side. Different sized wheels were put on to get extra speed. Air was forced through a tunnel at terrific speed into a chamber, where we placed our cooking pans, which we made out of old food tins from the food parcels. It was thought so powerful, it could burn earth.

German bread supplies were down to a seventh of a loaf per man. This we cut into thin slices to make it look more. The soup was made from potatoes and swedes, occasionally one could see a little meat floating on the surface.

German coffee came three times a day. Every two or three weeks, the cookhouse staff saved packets of raisins from the food parcels, and with some barley from the Germans we made a dish we all enjoyed. The cookhouse was run by the prisoners, but the guards or "ferrets", as we used to call them, kept a close eye on things.

The situation was getting worse food wise, with the chaps waiting outside the cookhouse for the vegetable peelings that had been thrown out. There was enthusiastic competition for the most succulent pieces, and to save a lot of bad feeling, each hut in turn collected them in a handcart. The cooks, being prisoners, threw out a great deal of good pieces with the peelings.

We were in tents at first, then in huts with the Americans later in the British compound. I was never in a position to help with escape attempts, always being in the background. "Dixie Dean" Slattery, Booth and others came round to each hut with the B.B.C. News. In the camp the names of the Escape Committee were kept secret.

Many books give details of life in the camps. This is my version of events as seen at the time. "No Flight from the Cage" was a good explanatory example.

I never shined in athletics, being slightly built, but cricket, football, basebell and ice skating were available. Most of my time was spent walking around the perimeter, thinking about my empty stomach, and wondering how the family were managing back home.

It was amazing how much equipment they had in the camp. A Scotsman managed to get hold of some Bag Pipes and he played them under the "poston boxes", driving the Germans crazy. I met a chap from the south of England who had been a prisoner for a couple of years. He was a wireless air gunner, and knew my home town of Harrogate very well. It was good to have someone to talk to when walking round the camp (time seemed to drag so much). Occasionally stalls were erected from old boxes, around the perimeter, and we could buy almost anything - watches, lighters, clothing and even food, but of course one had to have the cigarettes to barter with.

Contact was made with the farm workers, mostly Poles and Russians. When we first arrived at the camp the news spread around that 40,000 Russians had died of Typhus, and their graves were just behind the camp. Every few weeks we were de-loused (it sounds dreadful but it was a necessity). Almost everyone had trouble with "vermin". I have seen chaps checking their underwear for lice before they went to bed. They seemed to like the seams of garments. We had to strip in the shower room for our clothes to be heated up in ovens. We were also sprayed with "de-lousing powder".

The latrines were crude and in different sizes. If I remember correctly, at Heydekrug it was a hut, and inside were two long planks along each side. At intervals the planks were cut into circles, and that was it. There was no privacy. We all sat in a row, it was very embarrassing as most of the prisoners had some sort of stomach trouble. The Russian workers had the responsibility of cleaning them out when they were full.

At night before we turned in, our "blowers" were in operation all over the camp. The blowers were made from beaten out food tins, as with all our cooking utensils. One of the German food items was "Fish Cheese", gelatine with fish cheese inside, and made into a "fish cake". Most of the chaps wouldn't consider them because of the smell - it was horrible. I managed to get them down, and even bought more.

Another gift from the Germans were barrels of sauerkraut and "blue storks", a type of mushroom. They were all the colours of the rainbow, a yellow greenish slime - no thanks.

The Americans had an ingenious way of passing the time, managing to get some ice skates from Geneva. It was so cold, all that was necessary to make a skating ring was to throw buckets of water over the ground and it would freeze immediately. To pass the time, many of the Red Cross parcels were packed into chests made out of plywood, which were used to make gliders some seven feet long. The wood was split up and covered with toilet paper, and they really could fly, sometimes out of the compound. The German guards brought them back. After all, in some ways they were prisoners themselves. Any way we could entertain them was alright by them.

A school was started in the camp. The P.O.W.s came from all over the world, and many had been teachers in civy street. If you wanted to learn German, French or even Japanese, someone could help. Others were tradesmen, such as joiners, cabinet makers and painters. A theatre was made, and the stage, seats and so on were made by prisoners. Entertainers were available, and fine shows were staged. Even the Germans were in the audiences. Some of the men dressing up as women were so good that the lads waited outside the stage door to see them. (Just a bit of fun.)

Almost every day, we got the B.B.C. News through our secret radio. Also the German news, but we had to read between the lines for that. It was a well kept secret where the radio was, in pieces I think. Only a few knew.

Our camp leader, Dixie Dean, was liked by everyone, even the Germans. After the war he received the O.B.E. for his work in prisoner of war camps. He ended up being in charge of 12,000 men, Army and Air Force. The Committee came to each hut in turn, men were supplied to watch the windows to see there were no Germans about, then they read out the news. We heard about the 50 officers that had escaped from Sargan, and were captured and shot by the S.S. troops. It was the same night our aircraft was shot down, the 24th and 25th of March, 1944. Later we heard about the "Invasion of Europe". The German report was "Shot while trying to escape". It was a case of cold blooded murder. 70 prisoners escaped and many more were trapped in the tunnel. No-one who has not been a prisoner can comprehend the captives' mentality. Many writers have tried to explain it - it is doubtful if any of them succeeded. You are in the power of the enemy, you must obey his orders. although some P.O.W.s had a harder time than us, you still hear tales of German brutality. Here is one.

The Americans were caught trying to escape. They were ordered to raise their hands above their heads. A German officer deliberately placed his pistol against the ribs of one of the surrendered Americans, and pulled the trigger. Incredibly, the other man was spared to tell the tale of his murdered companion. He was buried in a shallow grave in the woods.

Shot while trying to escape - that was the excuse given by the Germans. We were completely at their mercy while trying to escape.
From a German magazine - While we were at Heydekrug, June the 6th 1944,

> *"The Invasion". During last night the enemy began his long-prepared "offensive" against Western Europe which has been awaited by us. Accompanied by heavy air attacks upon our coastal defences, he dropped airborne troops on the North West French Coast between Le Havre and Cherbourg, and undercover of strong Naval forces set troops ashore at several points along the coast. In this area of action bitter fighting is in progress."*

Rome had fallen on June the 2nd 1944, and the Germans started to use their "Flying Bombs".

Back to camp life.

Each hut in turn peeled the spuds in the kitchen. I didn't mind though and was quite an expert. Most of the chaps had dysentery while in the camp. We were so weak and vulnerable, much of our time was spent stretched out on our bunks. Sometimes we got up quickly and the room would start spinning. Malnutrition probably.

The main exercise we had was walking around the perimeter. It helped us to sleep at night. Each member of aircrew had a different story to tell, most were in the "Caterpillar Club" for having saved their lives by parachute.

Time seemed to drag after the invasion. We thought everything would be over very soon, but not so. We had an encounter with the Germans. Almost every day and night we had a roll-call to see if anyone had escaped during the night. One morning, a few of the chaps jumped out of bed and instead of getting dressed, they put overcoats over their nightclothes. The Commandant thought this was insulting, especially as one had his hands in his pockets. The officer saw him, pointed a finger at him and said "You, the Cooler", a sort of solitary confinement.

One day, we were all ordered out of our huts for roll-call on the parade ground. At each corner of the ground was a "Mauser Machine Gun" with helmeted German soldiers manning them. The guns were aimed at us. Our Commandant, a Prussian officer with a slight limp, came over followed by other officers to address the prisoners. He began by informing us that orders had been given from Berlin that reprisals were to be taken against all prisoners, in retaliation for the way German P.O.W.s had been treated out in the desert by the Allies (they were manacled). The Germans took our mattresses away and from then on we had to sleep on bare boards. The base of each bed consisted of slats of wood, which slotted in leaving gaps in between. So we had many sleepless nights. We heard on the grapevine that orders had been given by Hitler for all P.O.W.s to be executed and Himmler talked him out of it. Whether that is true or not has not been confirmed.

In the middle of the talk by the officer, someone started to "boo" in the true British spirit. We were taking a chance with all those machine guns pointing at us. Later everybody calmed down and we were dismissed. Back in the huts we found that the Germans had been searching, and had taken our mattresses and put them in another compound.

It was inevitable that someone would try to break through the wire and steal the mattresses back. Once that started to happen, the ball started to roll. Dozens of us went through the wire and carried our mattresses back. I was one of the last to go in, and was prevented from getting one. A German soldier came round the corner with a machine gun in his hand pointing at my back. We certainly went out quicker than we got in, expecting a bullet in the back. This episode was soon over and everything went back to normal. One way or another, danger was always around the corner for prisoners. The Germans were within their rights to shoot us. Afterwards, things were a bit vague, but somehow Dixie managed to get our mattresses back.

During the summer months it was very hot, enabling us to sun-bathe. The heat created a lot of whirlwinds, and if we left our clothes on the ground they would go whirling up in the air. V.I.P.s from Geneva (Red Cross) came and inspected the camp, and questioned the prisoners regarding their treatment. Although not a smoker, I had a few cigarettes to barter for food, and we also played cards. Winning would be more to bargain with. We used to get into groups and have discussions on almost any subject, mainly how the war was progressing. Airmen named Rod Mulally, Stephen Hughes and Killagrew were my constant companions. Two of my crew, Grant and McDonagh, were in a different part of the camp. However, we met occasionally.

As far as I can recall, McGillivary left Frankfurt and went straight to No.1 Officers Camp, staying there until the end of the war.

To keep myself warm, I made myself a sleeping bag out of an old blanket, having taught myself "Blanket Stitch", which came in very handy. Obtaining an old toothbrush, and shaping the end into a hook, made a crochet needle, and I used woollen garments that had been unravelled. Using the wool to make hats and berets, they certainly kept ones ears warm. I even made a vanity bag of wool, lined with the silk of my flying boots, and embroidered Pilots Wings on the front. Trying to make myself a pair of underpants was unsuccessful. My parachute would have been useful at this time, had it been available.

The Germans allowed all prisoners to have a diary, which came from Geneva. I suppose they hoped to get information from them. (We were wise to that.) I wrote rhymes and poems in mine, which I still have. Many were put in my first book, "Two Brothers At War", from the Army and Air Force. The Germans were always giving us pamphlets to read, in most cases it was propaganda, but one was rather different. It was obvious at the time that the Germans realised they were losing. The prisoners had been causing a lot of trouble by escaping and so on. The pamphlet stated, " Germany no longer treated escaping as a sport" and that Germany had been split up into "zones" and that any prisoner caught within these zones would be shot immediately.

After Germany declared war on Russia, the situation was reasonably quiet. Once the Russians got organised and were advancing, we had to move camp. The big guns flashed in the sky at night. They were only about twenty miles away. It's laughable really, when the Germans said "For you the war is over". We were seeing it first-hand, and in the weeks to come it was worse.

When the order came through to evacuate the camp, a load of food parcels arrived, and these were distributed. We were in no condition for marching. So many parcels had arrived, many were left behind for the advancing Russians, the German guards and even the civilians. On leaving, we were told to eat as much as possible and carry the rest.

At first the Germans wouldn't touch the food, not wanting to degrade themselves. After a while, they started to put tins of food in their haversacks. Everything else they destroyed before leaving the camp.

At this particular time, I lost touch with Grant and McDonagh.

All along the road lay discarded clothes and equipment. Only a limited amount could be carried. Some of the lads were fortunate enough to steal a handcart. This was loaded up with kit bags and other essentials. It was also handy if someone fell ill on the way. The people of Heydekrug were concerned there wouldn't be enough trains to evacuate them as they were being used by 3000 P.O.W.s. We were again herded into two cattle trucks for 36 hours. Eventually we were deep in Poland and ahead of us was Thorn. As we approached the camp, we passed many soldiers going to the front. Most of them were very young, as if they had been scraping the bottom of the barrel.

I remember very little about Thorn. When we first arrived we were told about the "Polish Land Girls" who entertained the prisoners by doing a striptease outside the barbed wire, dodging in and out of the bushes. The Germans soon put a stop to that.

Nearby was a Luftwaffe fighter station equipped with Fock Wolf 190s. Quite often they pretended to shoot up the camp, to frighten the life out of us. A large bridge was nearby. It was thought the "F.W.190s" patrolled the area to guard the bridge. We could see vapour trails in the sky, perhaps from rockets fired on England.

After a short while we had the "canary" or radio, and managed to get it working. Once again, as the Russians were advancing so fast, we had to be on the move again. It was now August 1944. We had only been here a few weeks.

Everywhere we travelled was countryside and woodlands. We bypassed all the big towns and cities. Most of the Americans leaving Heydekrug were marched to the coast and put into the hold of a ship. They must have had a horrific time. When put ashore, they were harassed by the "Hitler Youth" with fixed bayonets, prodding them and grabbing their kit, leaving it all by the roadside. It was said that some of the P.O.W.s were put in "dog cages" and were unable to stand up by themselves, from the treatment meted out to them.

We found out later that the Americans were taken to Sweinemunde on the Baltic Coast, and from there to Tychow in East Pomerania. It was said that when they were aboard the ship, food and water was not provided.

My life as a prisoner was reasonably comfortable compared to the rough treatment some had to suffer, notably the ones in Japanese hands. They suffered horrifically by comparison.

On our way to Fallingbostol in Germany by rail, we often had to stop in railway sidings while the raids were on. One night, Hanover was the target. The bomber streams flew overhead. We could see the vapour trails in the sky, and heard the bombs exploding.

There was much activity on the railways, with troops going to the front, and the wounded by repatriated. On arriving at Fallingbostol, we were offloaded into huts, around 70 to a hut. There was a long trestle table we used to eat from. Most of the men were in small groups, and between them they did all the work that was necessary. Our ration of bread was one seventh of a loaf per man per day. This we cut into small slices to stretch the ration provided.

The lavatories were the same as at Heydekrug, constructed of planks of wood with round holes provided to the appropriate size (no privacy at all). At times we even had to line up. Timber was in demand for the fires, and we didn't care where it came from. The Germans were careful not to leave any around. Huts were not safe.

 Kicking one piece of wood by one of the chaps, then another, and everyone wanted their share. Before long there was no sign that a hut ever existed.

Towards the end of 1944, raids on Germany hotted up in numbers of aircraft. Hundreds of Fortresses and Liberators left vapour trails in the sky, and both German and Allied fighters weaved in and out of the bomber streams. Planes were diving to earth, crews were baling out. "Ack Ack" guns were blazing away, a sight never seen in England.

12,000 prisoners were in the middle of it. When we were at Fallingbostol, Allied planes criss-crossed above us on the way to the main targets, such as Hanover, Hamburg, Stuttgart, Augsburg and Magdeburg.

When the temperature was high, many of us suffered from gastro-enteritis and dysentery. Except for half a parcel to each man, there were no more parcels from the Red Cross. The German rations were bread, potatoes and soup made of dried vegetables. We were deprived of our ration of one and a half spoonfuls of jam per man per week. Apparently the Allies had bombed the jam factory in Hamburg. If one had money or cigarettes (also the know-how) almost anything could be bought.

In fourteen months there was no bread or eggs. They were available, however, to those with cigarettes. Some German guards turned a blind eye. There were thousands of landworkers anxious to do deals, mostly the Russian and Polish workers who were forced to work.

Fallingbostol was an Army camp containing about 3000 prisoners. They didn't like the idea of another 3000 airmen arriving, especially as our leader, Dixie Dean took over, they would have to share their food. It was a large complex containing eight small compounds, with a complete circuit of over a mile. Walking around the perimeter was like having a ramble in the country.

We were housed in wooden huts, 24 to each hut, and for the first few days no mattresses were issued. Half a mile away was the cookhouse, which supplied our soup and coffee each day. It was difficult to move around because of the soft sand.

At this particular time we had no potato ration, but we did get Red Cross parcels which we had to share. As soon as the two services were integrated, stories were circulating of experiences in North Africa, Arnheme and Egypt. Some of the Army and Air Force were long standing prisoners.

Originally the huts were not locked, and some slept outside. An airman was shot by one of the guards, and from then on we were locked in.

"Enterprising" opened up Swap Shops where articles were bought and sold. Almost anything was available at a price. The guards were very helpful.

At this time, many of our camps had been overrun by the Russians, so it was time to move on again. The camp was evacuated, and with all our worldly goods we had collected, ready for a forced march. I believe we were issued with food parcels before leaving. I had my kit bag, small case and the sleeping bag I had made, together with what was left of my food parcel. It was very bulky as I also carried an overcoat.

About 300 prisoners were left behind to be repatriated on medical grounds. A few lads hid in the deserted camp, hoping to make an escape when we had all left. After leaving Heydekrug I lost touch with Grant and McDonagh. Later I was told McDonagh was one of the 300 who were repatriated, and was back in England before the war was over.

After a few days' marching, all our food had been eaten. We were starving now, and had to manage on what the German guards could scrounge for us. We were more or less living off the land. The German guards did their best for us as we were on the march. We must remember thay were starving as well, and just as much prisoners as we were.

They stopped mostly at villages and farms, where the farmers were ordered to open their "clamps of potatoes". Sometimes, after a hard day, we were given a few potatoes that had been cooked. Sugar beet was tried, after frying it first to remove the tarty taste. On occasions we did get turnip or swede soup.

Those who were able to speak a little German had a better chance of bartering for food. As near as I can recall, we were on the march for about four weeks before we were released. It was amazing the different places we stayed at overnight. All around us fighting was taking place, and at night we were almost completely surrounded by gun flashes on the skyline.

It seemed as if we were in a horseshoe shape. As soon as one army advanced we retreated one way, and another would catch us up, so we retreated again. It was hopeless, but still the Germans wouldn't release us.

To give you some idea of the position we were in, as we approached the River Elbe, an attempt was made to cross one of the main bridges. On one side of the bank were "Ack Ack" guns manned by the "Hitler Youth". They shouted "Two Spitfires", which were flying high up. They ran in a panic, and jumped into a trench, shouting "Achtung, Achtung, Spitfire." Their guns were not fired. Maybe they had no ammunition left. There must have been at least 1000 prisoners in this column, dragging their feet along the road. They straightened up, and started to sing as they marched along. At that moment, I was proud to be British.

We reached the bridge and crossed it. About twenty minutes later the Germans blew it up. We saw the explosion in the distance. When the war was over we crossed again, by lorry, this time over a "Pontoon Bridge" made by the Army engineers.

One night, after a long day's march, we stopped at a large farm. The Germans decided we would spend the night there. It was only natural that the men would try to get the best spots to rest. Plenty of straw was available, so most of the men went up into the loft. The place I chose was near the entrance of a barn. In the evening when the men had eaten whatever food they could scrape together, the barn doors were shut. It was dark inside, and during the early hours of the morning, the inevitable happened, there being no way anyone could get out to go to the toilet. The men down below were complaining about the wet coming from above. Luckily I was near the door.

I'd been poorly all day, feeling sick and with a splitting headache. Claustrophobia had returned. I struggled over the sleeping men to get to the doors, and knocked until a German soldier opened the doors. I put my hand to my forehead, and pointed to the floor outside the door. Although the soldier carried a rifle, he did not stop me when I lay on the ground.

I did manage to sleep a little, but next morning I felt a little stupid and uncomfortable. There was a channel outside the door which ran into a drain. This was the place the lads had used before going into the barn. I didn't care, the way I felt at that moment.

On another two occasions when we were on the march around the country, I felt a little uncomfortable when I visited a smaller latrine similar to the one at Heydekrug. The latrine was empty fortunately. I chose one of the seats and sat down. I was relaxed until an old woman walked in. Although there was plenty of room in the hut, she sat next to me. (She probably wanted the company.)

When we were somewhere in Germany, in the countryside, and on the march, several of the chaps wanted to relieve themselves. In the middle of a field a rectangular trench had been dug. Two posts had been driven into the ground at each end, and across was a pole. That was it. We had to balance on the pole to go to the toilet. Just our luck - a group of women walked by laughing their heads off, all they could see was a row of bare bottoms.

We marched for about an hour and then had ten minutes rest. We were so tired we just collapsed. The difficulty was trying to get mobile again. One of the nights we spent in a wood. This was an easy way for the Germans to guard us, keeping us together. I chose a comfortable spot under a tree to spend the night, but just my luck - it rained all night. Consequently, next morning I looked like a drowned rat.

On our travels, while on the march, scattered all over the landscape were wrecks of German and Allied aircraft. Whilst passing some airfields, it was clear the planes looked in perfect condition. However, fuel was not available for them.

Due to our predicament, Dixie Dean persuaded the Commandant to drive to Lubeck, where there was a store of food parcels. It was announced later that the food parcels were on the way by truck. In the village of Gresse on the 19th of April 1945, columns of P.O.W.s from the neighbouring areas arrived for their share of the food parcels. Each man was issued with two. 12,000 men were in and around this village.

We were told by Dixie Dean to take the parcels out of the village before opening them up. (We couldn't wait.) Two parcels in addition to all our kit was much too heavy to carry. Besides my extra clothes, overcoat and sleeping bag, I also had a kit bag and an attache case. We consumed as much food as we could and kept some, the rest was discarded along the route. The American food parcels contained a very unsavoury tin of food, "Olio Margarine". It was terrible. Tins of it were thrown away, even the Germans didn't like it.

I saw Grant a few times while we were on the march. McDonagh was still at Fallingbostol. The B.B.C. kept us informed with the news at home, courtesy of the home-made Camp Radio (canary).

Many Allied aircraft were in the vicinity regularly, and when R.A.F. Typhoons suddenly appeared, it wasn't unusual. However, an attack by them was a complete and awesome surprise, causing havoc with our column of prisoners, resulting in many casualties. Our group was in the middle of the column, and the aircraft seemed to be attacking us; I dived for cover in a ditch at the side of the road. One of my companions was a soldier, another was R.A.F. Although there was no protection in actual fact, I put the case on my head. The kitbag covered my back, and the food parcel covered my legs. It is surprising what people will do under stress.

My head was pressed into the ground, as the planes used "anti-personnel" bombs and rockets. The "thud thud" of the cannon shells all around could be heard, also explosions. Seven of the aircraft were circling round for another attack when the eighth realised a mistake had been made and waved to us. How these pilots must have felt, knowing what they had done! No German planes were about, no guns were firing at them, they had no excuse.

In a few seconds it was all over. Getting up from the ground, the first person I saw was an Army sergeant. His face was covered in blood, he was screaming in pain. Carnage was all around me. Shrapnel penetrated through the case which was on my head. The airman next to me was wounded in the abdomen and looked as if he was finished. I certainly had a Guardian Angel that day. 33 P.O.W.s were killed outright, 42 were injured, 22 seriously. Quite a few died later. Seven German guards were killed. Some of the chaps, Army and Air Force, had been prisoners for 3 or 4 years, only to be killed by our own people! Dixie, with help from others, dug a mass grave and buried the casualties. The Germans did the best they could for the wounded, but they did not have the necessary medical equipment. Shock and gangrene killed many.

Pilot Van Slyke and myself.

Engineer Whitelaw and mid-upper gunner Grant

Warrant Officer Harry Ball, April 1945

FROM LEFT TO RIGHT: Mrs Agnes Ball, Eric Boutillier (Best Man), Harry Ball,

Doris Ball (nee Swain), Ron Swain, Irene Swain

Mid upper gunner,
Grant and his wife

Bomb aimer,
McDonagh and his wife

Navigator,
McGillivary and his wife

After this unfortunate episode, Dixie asked the Commandant for permission to go through the German lines, in an attempt to prevent the Allies killing our own people. He was given a signed letter to get through. Dixie had been using an old bicycle to get around from column to column, trying to help where he could. He obtained a better bike from a German officer. He also promised the Commandant he would return. After this catastrophe was over, it was back to marching again. Some of the chaps were having stomach ailments, having eaten too much too soon, in addition to being in poor health.

Dixie was accompanied by an interpreter. It was risky travelling through the German lines, as there were many S.S. Troops about who would shoot without warning. He was successful, and was taken to the British officer who was in charge. He explained that Typhoons had attacked P.O.W.s on the march. The officer said "It is fortunate they had been warned!" Another strike was arranged for the next day. The officer said "I suppose you will be going home now." Dixie replied "No, I promised the German Commandant I would return."

List of British Personnel killed by low flying Aircraft at Gresse

April 19th 1945

Interred at Gresse churchyard

	P.O.W. No	Rank	Name	Service	Nationality
1		L/Sgt	L H J Goodfellow	2571861	British
2	1094/Luft 6	F/Sgt	K Mortimer	1431168 RAF	British
3	1093	Sgt	E Bardsley	RAF	British
4		Sgt	J S Breytenbach	UDF	S Africa
5	25505	Cpl	Downie	Cameronians	British
6	*5904/Thorn	Cpl	G Moir	28745614	British
7	20386	Cpl	P M Paton	918030	British
8	430	W/O	J Gage	RAF	British
9	3932/viiia	Pte	R Woodgate		Australian
10	29815/viiib		Unknown		
11	25731/11d		A G Hunt	East Scotish	Canadian
12	26387/viiib		Unknown		
13	3263/Luft 6	Sgt	W E Lawton	RAF 1565563	British
14	138572 x 1a		Unknown		
15	3566/Luft 6	F/Sgt	J Gibbs	RAF	British
16	2121/Luft 3	Sgt	S J Wheadon	RAF	British
17	918	W/O	Shierlaw	RAAF	Australian
18	39152	W/O	F B Duffield	RAF 647048	British
19	874/Luft 6	W/O	W E Mackenzie	RCAF R/65193	Canadian
20	13064/viiib	W/O	W P J Watson	RAF	British
21	24384	W/O	C W Heathman	RAF 1378655	British
22		W/O	G Douglass	RCAF	Canadian
23			Joyce	East Scotish	Canadian
24	994	W/O	K A Fox	RCAF R/126002	Canadian
25	24510/viiib	Sgt	L B H Hope	RNZAF	New Zealand
26	941	Sgt	Hawkins	RAF	
27	3429/Luft 6	F/Sgt	D Bauldie	RAF	British
28	9669/viiib	W/O	Claydon	RAF	
29	335/Luft 3	W/O	G A Losh	RAF 623752	British
30	143/iiie	W/O	W A Bond	RAF	

plus three who died in hospital (indicated with x on next page)

List of men taken to hospital with injuries following aircraft attack

	P.O.W. No	Rank	Name	Service
1	1256	W/O	L D E Marriott	658181
2	138531	W/O	C L Williams	546575
3	7769	Cpl	G Mensies	46196
4	1632	Sgt	J Whitehouse	1442553
5	3902	Cpl	F H Surman	VX6250
6	42771	W/O	C A Chambers	NZ416213
7	89	Sgt	J Foster	645044
8	338	A C	J D Stuart	639318
9	29612	Cpl	R Richardson	4627848
10	486	W/O	H Buchanan	404646
11	24336	W/O	D Cotsell	567496
12	109	W/O	R Bonson	635808
13	7798	Cpl	G Maman	SX4930
14	8696		R H Reed	6286965
15	601		Ridgeway	338706
16	199		J Lee	160352
17	32003		Mackay	2930106
18	8801		Turrell	S1054811
19	78		Austin	746906
20	279575		Pix *	2722115
21	3385		Barnell *	1853402
22	12274		A Brown *	746717
23	1029		G A C Read *	1186489
24	25604		R R Toillon *	L12077
25	512 x	W/O	Mckenna *	11489
26	33243	Sgt	Worthy *	5492295
27	50392		Brooks *	622115
28	431		Lowman *	570626
29	46	F/Sgt	I Farquhar *	710102
30	23246		Walters *	7419
31	448 x		Steele *	RAF
32	70845		Copley *	3252915
33	39166	W/O	Bailey *	922923
34	14065	Sgt	Gabain *	2360079
35	315	Sgt	Knoter *	787548
36	29465	Pte	Glynn-Baker *	
37	29506	Cpl	Glynn-Baker	
38	200	Cpl	D Patterson *	722234
39	10049	Sgt	C Bolden *	nx9137
40	1615 x	F/Sgt	F T Price *	1509811
41	3469	F/Sgt	S A C Smith *	180695
42	9659	W/O	Lord *	955266
43	31090	Bdr	J H Webber *	51205
44	175	F/Sgt	R A Hunt *	1699818
45	442	W/O	V Rose *	1111501

* = Seriously injuried

x = Subsequently died (burried at Gresse)

The Army O.C. could not understand this, not knowing Dixie Dean. After that, life seemed much the same. We marched across Luneburg Heath (where eventually the Armistice was signed) and from village to village. Food was scarce. We relied on the generosity of the Germans.

News came through that Taffy Gibbs and five other members of his group were all killed at Gresse.

Two of us left the column and went into a village hoping to scrounge food. At one house the occupants were asked if they had any food to spare, and they gave us a glass of what looked like sour milk. It didn't look very appetising but we drank it anyway.

Last few days and release.
Soon after leaving the house two guards appeared and challenged us with their rifles. Luck was with us - they did not fire, but escorted us back to the column. The war was coming to a close so it wasn't worth the risk of escaping. One futile and lucky example - two men escaped from the column and were caught by the German Army, therefore facing a firing squad. Dixie, hearing of the incident, intervened and saved their lives. All this time the BBC was coming through with the news. The last few days before release were pretty hectic, especially as far as Dixie was concerned. In addition to getting help from the Allied Army, and warning them of our presence in the area, he saved lives in other ways.

Approximately two hundred German crack S.S. troops had gathered in a village, and were going to fight to the last man. Dixie made contact. Somehow in his enterprising way he convinced the Senior Officer how futile it was to carry on fighting - he surrendered to Dixie. We were wandering around the countryside like sheep, stopping when we were told to, and eating when food was available. On the last day I happened to be with an Australian. He was almost bald - I think he must have given the wrong age when he joined up. He was showing me how to make a log fire - Australian style - by laying one end of a log into the centre of the fire. As soon as it starts to burn push it further in, adding a few more logs in the same way - it makes a decent fire. We were still discussing the fire when an Army Sergeant, who was standing near us said "Look - Churchill Tanks". They were coming across the field. I was relieved to know that they were ours. The German who was guarding us certainly did - he threw his rifle, overcoat and belt to the ground and disappeared.

I grabbed the belt as a souvenir . On the buckle was written "Gott Mit Uns" (God be with us). The tanks were part of Montgomery's 8th Army. We were free!.

When we were first captured the Germans took away our watches and lighters. When the Allied Army were putting German prisoners into compounds they were searched first, our lads giving a helping hand. Some considered that they were justified in helping themselves to some items, as their valuables were filched in similar circumstances when they were captured.

Eventually we arrived at an airport - I have no idea whether it was in France or Germany. Large tents had been erected by the Red Cross. As we entered a cup of tea was given to us together with white bread, the first since incarceration - it was like cake! After a few hours' rest some American Dakotas landed to take the Americans away. It seemed a long wait for us, and naturally we were impatient to meet our loved ones. The RAF had called on the Squadrons for volunteers to bring us back. Before long Lancasters started to arrive. It was my first trip in a Lancaster. Even though, out of necessity, we had to sit on the floor, we were very grateful. On landing at RAF Cosford we were debriefed, deloused, given a meal, and had our photo taken - I wish I had that photo now.

On my way home at last.
We were all scruffy, many with beards including myself. Home leave was next on the agenda. This was an experience that could never be completely forgotten, even after 50 years. Some of the chaps were in a shocking condition and had lost weight. My weight had remained stable since enlistment in 1941 - 9 stone 2lbs.

Most of the V.E.Day celebrations had finished when I returned to Harrogate. We were alive though, unlike many of our comrades. I saw two of the crew before they embarked for Canada - McDonagh and McGillivary. I also saw Grant prior to his return home to Scotland. This completes my story, to the best of my memory, which has faded somewhat over half a century. A lot of the chaps who were in a bad way went straight to hospital, and were given extra food rations. Brother Fred stopped flying in June 1945 and was posted to Cardington, working with new recruits. Later he was posted to Wilmslow near Manchester, doing the same job. As it happened my future wife did her training there when she first joined the WAAFs in September 1945. Fred was Administration Officer at the time. He did not start flying again until 1949. My sister Marjorie married her Canadian boyfriend, and they had a baby girl. Both Marjorie and her friend Betty Dunn were "war brides" and left England for Canada in January 1946.

While I was away Harrogate had filled up with Americans. I had my share of them in East Prussia. Anyway they had all gone when I arrived home. At the end of my leave in June 1945 I was posted to Church Fenton in Yorkshire - Reception and Disposal for RAF POWs. Every man had a code number, depending on how many years he had been in the Service. My number was 41, and at that moment they were releasing up to 36, so I had to await my turn. We were asked whether we would like to sign up for a commission, but we would have to sign on for another three years. I felt that there was no future in the RAF for me. After serving for four and a half years, the sooner I got back to Civvy Street the better. It was another six months before I was released. On 13th May 1945 I became a Warrant Officer, not a commissioned rank but the next best thing. At least I had worked my way up from the ranks.

My next posting was to Redruth in Cornwall, an isolated place like the prison camp I had just come out of. When I reported for duty the Officer in Charge there - "You, as a POW, should have been released long ago. In any case the Station is closing down". Three weeks after I had left Church Fenton, the group had gone up to 46 - as my number was 41 I should have been released straight away. There was nothing for me to do down there, so I spent most of my time in the Handicraft section making handbags. The RAF supplied the materials and tools and showed me how to make them, and that was it. I became quite good at it and took several bags home with me. There was one thing I had learnt and that was patience.

Waiting to be Demobbed.
After a few weeks I was posted to 16MU Stafford on a motor

mechanics' course, which I thought would be useful to me in Civvy Street. Grant, my MU gunner who lived in Scotland, wrote to me and said that a friend of his who had the same group number as myself had been released, so I went to the Adjutant and told him this, and asked for my release. He regretted that he could do nothing until it came through on DROs (Daily Routine Orders). It did - six months later.

As fate would have it, had I been released earlier I would not have met my future wife Doris. When I first arrived in camp I met another W.O. - he was aircrew but not a POW. When we had got our billets fixed up we decided to see what the town had to offer. I had a motor bike with me, which was handy to run around on, In town we asked one of the locals which was the best pub. Doris, who had just joined up and done her six weeks' training, was posted to Stafford on the same day as myself. She was with another WAAF and had gone to the same pub, and sat down next to my friend and myself. My mate soon got into conversation with them. I was a bit shy in those days, hardly speaking a word, but we enjoyed ourselves. I took Doris back to camp on my motor bike, with the agreement of my mate, and dropped her off at the Guard Room. I had fallen for her straight away, but it was a long time before she felt the same way about me. I asked her for a date and she said Yes, but never expected me to turn up, but of course I did. From then on between duties we went out together. I was a dull person and didn't dance, whereas Doris had won prizes for dancing. She smoked but I did not. She was only 18 and I was 5 years older. Doris was a bit on the flighty side, and I was just the opposite. I think the motor bike was the attraction.

I started my duties as Motor Mechanic, and as I had no experience I had to take orders from lower ranks (LACs) who had learnt their trade. The trouble was that the RAF took advantage of this. I was really an LAC Wireless Operator with a W.O.rank learning to be a motor mechanic. Yet I still had my W.O. duties to do e.g. Witnessing Officer on pay parades. Hundreds of personnel - F/Sgts, Sgts, Cpls, ACs and WAAFs - all waited in rows to be paid. When their names were called out I had to check the pay they were given, all very tiring on the eyes. Another job was Orderly Officer, which involved walking round the Mess at mealtimes and asking if there were any complaints. Nobody told me what to do if there were any -

I would have to use my own initiative.

In the hangar where I worked we had a roll-call every morning. All ranks lined up and their names were taken. The trouble was that I was in charge of the roll-call one morning as a W.O., and the next morning I was in the squad and my name was taken by a Sgt.

The last few weeks of my service.
Once when Doris and I came back from a weekend in Harrogate we were late in getting back to camp, and the Sgt. in charge of the roll-call put me down as absent. The next was that I was put on a charge by a Sgt. and had to go in front of the Commanding Officer. As soon as he saw me he said "What are you doing here?" and told me to clear off. What most people did not know was that I could not be put on a charge by a Sgt. Only an Air Commodore could put me on a charge or Court Martial, and we did not have one at Stafford. By this time I was getting a bit fed up, and I wanted to get back home and start a new life as painter and decorator.

Most of the work that we did at Stafford was done in hangars - reboring the engines of lorries (Dodges and Studebakers), and even working on motor-bikes and sidecars. We used to have fun riding them around the hangars. This work would be of some use to me in Civvy Street. One weekend in Harrogate, after I had had a few drinks, I asked Doris to marry me. I don't think she believed me at first, but anyway she said " Yes". On leave in Wolverhampton I bought her an engagement ring. It was called a "double diamond twist". Doris applied for her demob because we wanted to get married. She was asked to give a date so she picked a Saturday out of the blue, Feb.16th, which was my birthday. We were married in uniform at Knaresborough Registry Office. I had already got her parents' consent when I went down to London. In one week Doris was a civilian. She stayed with her parents until I got my demob, and then we went back to Harrogate to live with my mother. It was time to forget about the war, and to think about starting work, and maybe starting a family.

Meeting my crew and other famous people.

From 1946 to approx.1982 all my time and energy was spent on the family, and building up a good business - H Ball and Sons, Decorators.

I retired in 1982 when I was 60, and from then on I have been in touch with several RAF clubs, and met a lot of famous people, I went to Canada to see my sister Marjorie. Also saw McDonagh and McGillivary - they were all keeping well. McDonagh was having a bit of trouble with his underpants - every so often pieces of metal would stick out of the side of his leg, making a hole in his pants. He was the one that was badly wounded. We had quite a long talk about what had happened to him while he was a prisoner.

The first club I went to was Hendon, to a luncheon given by the Irvin Parachute Co. for the Caterpillar Club, out of loyalty to Mr Irvin who founded the Club in 1926. Membership of this club is very exclusive - you must have had your life saved by baling out. Parachutes were originally made of silk from the caterpillar, hence the name. Mr Irvin's family decided to get all the Caterpillar members together, about 300 at a time, to attend a dinner. By now there must be about 10,000 members.

I met a lot of Halifax flyers, one from 158 Squadron, and a Spitfire pilot who had done 300 sorties. It was strange to see all those ageing men, most with bald heads like mine. We were all between 60 and 70. While I was there, two pilots whose lives had been saved by parachutes, by ejecting from a jet plane, received their Caterpillars. Someone in the hall shouted "Now that you've got one flaunt it!" A great time was had by all.

In September 1982 I was invited by the Aircrew Association to attend a banquet at the Guildhall in London, to honour Sir Arthur Harris on his 90th birthday. He was Commander-in-Chief of Bomber Command from 1942 to 1945, and the man who organised the 1000 bomber raids. Talk about famous people, the following are a few of those who attended.

Sir Arthur Harris Bart OBE, DSO, AFC, LLD (Air Chief Marshall)
Air Vice Marshall Bennett CB, DSO, CBE, FRAes (Pathfinder Force)
Group Captain Sir Douglas Bader CBE, DSO, DFC (Fighter Pilot) (POW)
Group Captain Cheshire VC, OM, DSO, 2 BARS, (Dam Busters)
Air Chief Marshall Sir Augustus Walker GCB, CBE, DSO, DFC, AFC
Air Marshall Sir John Curtiss KCB, CBM
Rear Admiral Querits CB, OBE, DSO
Air Chief Marshall Sir Christopher Foxley-Norris GCB, KCB, CB, DSO, OBE
Colonel McBride (Canadian Adviser)
Air Commodore Probert MBE, MA
Group Captain Laycock (Vulcan Bombers Waddington)
Group Captain Bygate (New Zealand Defence Staff)
Colonel Alderman (U.S.A.)
Sir Ronald Gardner-Thorpe CBE, TD, DCL, DH
Lord Mayor of London
Miss Lettice Curtis (ATA Pilot)
Colonel Walbrecht USAF, UK
Wing Commander Squire AFC (RAF Wittering)
Air Commodore Pack CBE (RAF Strike Command)
Squadron Leader Jackson MBE
Air Marshall Sir Edward Chilton KBE, CB
Group Captain Tait DSO and 2 bars, DFC and bar, ADC (617 Dambusters)
Group Captain Hamish Mahaddie DSO, DFC, C Eng, AFRes (Pathfinders)
Mrs Hortense Daman Clew, Belgian Res.Worker (Helped airmen escape)
Sqadron Leader Shannon DSO, DFC (617 Dambusters)

And plenty more. Can you imagine me amongst that lot - a mere W.O. Both my brother and I were retired and so were able to attend a lot of these clubs, including the RAFA Club, Air Crew Assoc., 158 Squadron Club, POW Club, Caterpillar Club, Polish A.F.Club, Nottingham and York Air Crew Assoc.

When I went to the 158 "do" for the first time it was just after the Falklands War. At Brize Norton I met my old Signals leader Sandy Sandal. He remembered Van Slyke's crew, also Raymond Lister

who was our spare navigator on our first trip to Berlin. .
that my skipper had a reputation for killing off naviga
true, we only lost one.

It was from Brize Norton that most of the transport was sen,
Falklands. We were shown around the hangars, and saw all t   -g
planes, after which we had our reunion dinner. As I write this
I have just heard that Dixie Dean, our camp leader, has died.
Thousands of people will remember him - he was one in a million.
Our next reunion dinner was at Grosvenor House, Park Lane,
London with the Aircrew Association. This was the best of the RAF
reunions. I got a "once in a lifetime" photo with Sir Arthur Harris
sitting on a chair, Sir Michael Beetham standing next to him
on his right, and myself on his left with my hand on Harris's
shoulder. All the big names were there including several VCs,
one Air Marshall, 3 Air Vice-Marshalls, 2 Air Chief Marshalls,
a Brigadier General, 2 Wing Commanders, one Major, 3 Group
Captains, and many more.

In November 1983 we went to the Lords Banqueting Centre in
London with the POW Assoc. When I heard these famous people
from America and the Commonwealth countries speaking from a
platform only a few yards away from me, I realised how lucky I was
to be there. When we were down at Lords, Dixie Dean came over
to our table. He was in a wheel chair as he was suffering from
multiple sclerosis. His wife, who came from Harrogate, was with
him. Meeting him again was marvellous. It is good to talk about
old times. This is the end of my story.

Harry Ball.

was a letter from my Commanding Officer to say that I
ad been reported missing.

158S/C.452/89/P1

No.158 Squadron Royal Air Force
25th March 1944

Dear Mrs Ball

It is with the greatest regret that I have to write confirming the news, given in my telegram of today, that your son Harry Ball has been reported missing from an operational sortie against Berlin on the night of 24/25th March 1944. The aircraft in which your son was wireless operator took off at 18.50hrs on 24th March 1944. Since then nothing has been heard. There is of course a possibility that the crew may have landed safely, but it is too early to expect any news of such an eventuality. Should I hear anything I will communicate with you immediately. It is desired to explain that the request in the telegram, notifying you of the casualty, was included with the object of avoiding his chance of escape being prejudiced by undue publicity, in case he was still at large. This is not to say that any information about him is available, but is a precaution in the case of all personnel reported missing.

I am enclosing a list of the names and addresses of the next of kin of the rest of the crew, in case you wish to communicate with them.

Your son's personal effects are being collected, and will be sent to the Standing Committee of Adjustment, Colnbrook, Slough for onward transmission to you in due course. If you should wish to make any enquiry regarding your son's effects, will you please address it to the Effects Officer, RAF Station Driffield, East Yorkshire. May I, on behalf of myself and the Squadron as a whole, extend to you our sincere sympathy and understanding at this anxious time.

Yours Sincerely
Wing Commander, Commanding
No.158 Squadron R.A.F.

"Arn't Men Beasts !"

The dreaded telegram.

Mrs A.Ball
18 Mount Parade
Harrogate
Yorkshire
The first telegram arrived on 25th March to say that I was reported missing. In June, 3 months later, a second telegram arrived to say that I was a prisoner in German hands.

What a strain it must have been for the parents of all those that were in the same position. At least Mother knew then that I was still alive.

Much to my disapointment, my Flying Log Book was destroyed in 1960. I was told that this was because I never claimed it. It should have been sent home after I was taken prisoner.

Letters to my mother from the mothers of crew members.

Mrs A.Ball   Central Butte
18 Mount Parade   Saskatchewan
Harrogate   Canada
Yorkshire

                                                      18th June 1944

Dear Mrs Ball,

We are happy to tell you that Allan is a Prisoner of War. We do hope you have had the same good news of your son. We know things won't be pleasant for them, but at least they are alright, and the Red Cross are so good about providing food and clothing for them.

We have had a letter from Mrs McDonagh saying Norman is a prisoner too, so we feel sure the rest of the crew are alright. The war is really going ahead lately, and surely old Hitler will see the trap approaching. It will be a happy day when it is all over. Hoping to hear good news from you soon, I am yours sincerely

Mrs McGillivary   (My navigator's mother)

I told you she was geared too high . . . !

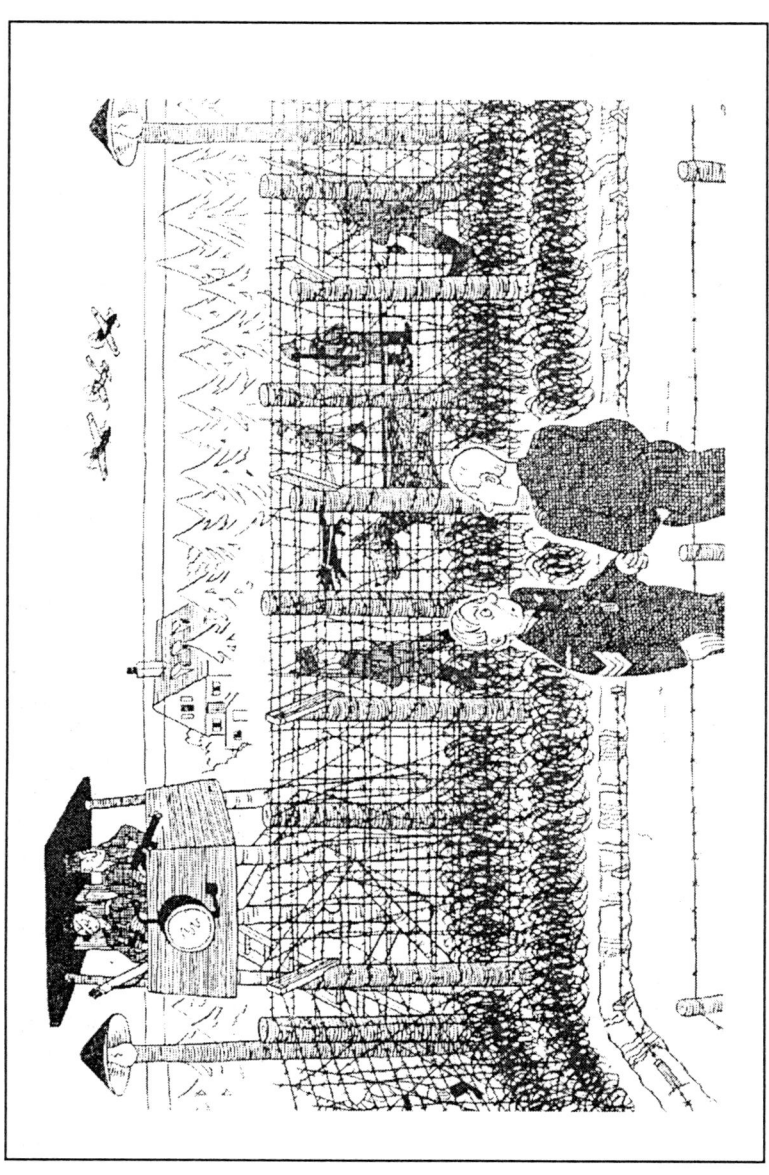

"Wait till he looks the other way, then you hop over the wire . . . . !"

Dear Mrs Ball and Marjorie,

I am writing this note to both of you at once - I hope you will excuse
me. I got your lovely letters and thanks so much for them. It does
seem nice to hear from the people who knew Allan. We seem to
have so much in common, as Harry and Allan are the only two not
heard from. Time seems so long - over four months since that fatal
trip. Surely if they had lost their lives they would have been found
and reported long before this. They may be in hiding somewhere,
we can still hope and pray.

We are so thankful to know that four out of the seven are
prisoners, Some day they will be home, and can tell us of that
perilous trip. Mrs Grant (mid upper gunner's mother) tells me they
had a hard trip in Jan. The crew baled out when they reached the
English coast. Allan never told us anything - only that they
got along OK. Allan's girl, Winnie Curran, wrote and said that
Kenneth Marsden-Mowbray is presumed dead. I had a letter from
his wife, but he was still missing when she wrote. She is expecting
a wee one in September. Poor dear girl. She sent me a little picture
of them both. Thanks so much for Harry's picture, it is lovely, and
we know which one is Harry - we have such a nice picture ofjust he
and Allan. I also had a nice letter from Mrs Whitelaw (engineer's
mother) and Mrs Grant, also Mrs McGillivary. They spoke so nicely
of Allan.

I do hope, Marjorie, that you are happily married, and that you will
come back to Canada after this cruel war is over. I surely wish
Allan could bring Harry back with him, as he did like him so much.
I also hope your other brother is fine. Our son Donald was in
hospital in Italy with an abscess on his hip. He said he read a book
each day, so he wasn't very sick. He does write cheerful letters.
Now Mrs Ball, this will be all for tonight. We'll have to keep in
touch, and keep smiling for the rest of the family, and hope and
pray for our lads who are away. Yours most truly,

Addie Van Slyke
(Mother of the pilot)

" Have you been here long ? "

It was something of a shock to the older prisoners, of from four
to five years standing, to see youngsters of nineteen or twenty,
who were still at school during the early years of the war,
arriving in the camp.

This last letter was sent after my parents had received word that I was a POW.

Central Butte
Saskatchewan
Canada

20th August 1944

Dear Mrs Ball,

I was so glad to hear that your son was a prisoner of war. While it may not be so pleasant, it is a wonderful feeling to know that they are alive and well. We have had a few letters from Allan. Of course he can say very little, but it is nice to receive word in his own writing. We are still waiting to hear from Mrs Van Slyke - they have had no official word of their son yet. It is hard to have to wait so long. We hope they will soon be home now, and then they will be able to tell us all about it. It is two years since Allan was last home - the time does get very long. The war is really getting ahead now. Surely the Germans won't be able to last out much longer.

We are very busy with the harvest now. The cutting of wheat is in full swing - the crops are lovely this year The girls were all home the first two weeks in July, but we have just three home now. Gladys the married girl stays with us - her husband is in England with the R.C.A.F. I believe he is stationed not far from where you live - not far from Hull. The other girls at home are twelve and eight years old. Norma is in the R.C.A.F. Alice teaches at school, and Irene keeps books for a store.

Allan is in Stalagluft 1 - is that where your boy is? Mrs McDonagh's boy is at Dulagluft, so the crew are widely seperated. I received a letter from Mrs Mowbray (Rear gunner's wife) saying that her husband is believed killed. There are so many broken hearts. It does seem too bad that such things have to be. I will be glad to hear from you frequently - we like to keep in touch with you.
Sincerely yours

Mrs John McGillivary

It is amazing how long it took for information to come through from the Red Cross - in our case three months. Even then most of the news was not up to date. In one letter it was said that the crew had seperated from one another. This happened only in the case of McGillivary - because he was an officer he went straight to Stalagluft 1. The main officers' camp was Stalagluft 3 Sargon. He stayed at No.1 until the end of the war when he was released. McDonagh, after he came out of a Berlin hospital, Grant and myself went to Stalagluft 6, Heydekrug, East Prussia.

Van Slyke, Mowbray and Whitelaw went down with the plane - they were unable to get out. Although aircrew underwent a lot of stress, most of us didn't feel it at the time. It was the wives and families who bore the brunt, not knowing what had happened to us.

Letter from Mr Chorley, author of "158 squadron - In Brave Company"

Dear Harry,

I was absolutely delighted to receive your letter, in which you recorded a quite graphic account of your final operation with 158 Squadron, plus odds and ends concerning your operational tour. In the revised account of the Squadron's history I shall certainly include extracts from your most interesting letter. I have looked at my notes, taken some years ago when I first researched the Squadron's records. This is what I have recorded concerning the operation to Berlin on 24/25th March, Zero Hour 22.30hrs - The attack will comprise of 830 aircraft, operating in five waves,(the actual number of bombers dispatched totalled 810) the Squadron being detailed to fly in the second and third waves.

2nd wave will bomb 22.33 to 22.36 made up from B.D.E.C.H.L.N.

3rd wave will bomb 22.36 to 22.39 made up from C.K.M.P.R.S.U.V.T.

In the event"R" did not take off, so leaving 15 crews as follows:-

HX349.G ....F/Sgt.J.Hitchman
HX340.N ....P/O R.A.Gray R.C.A.F.
LV790.L ....P/O M.V.Lawrence R.C.A.F.
HX334.C ....F/Sgt.B.D.Bancroft R.C.A.F.
LV917.H ....S/Ldr.W.J.Wellor
HX322.B ....P/O E.G.Strange
LW658.K ....F/O W.A.Hughes R.C.A.F.
LV920.D ....F/L J.N.Reynolds
LW722.U ....F/Sgt.A.J.S.Wright R.C.A.F.
LV792.E ....F/Sgt.G.W.Johnson
LW635.M ....F/Sgt.P.Kettle-Roy
LW634.P ....F/Sgt.S.Hughes
LW721.S ....F/Sgt.A.R.Van Slyke R.C.A.F.
LW718.T ....P/O K.S.Simpson R.C.A.F.

As you know "S" was lost, and now that I have your letter I
will be able to report what happened. Poor Simpson struggled for
home with failing engines, and reached the English coast, only to
force-land in an off-shore minefield, hit a mine and explode. What a
cruel stroke of luck. Of the rest some survived, but sadly many
fell in the operations of April/May 1944. S.Hughes went down
at Nuremburg, and W.A.Hughes and Kettle-Roy on the second
Tergnier raid. Both were   disastrous. Lawrence also went down.

Extracts from Volkischer Beobachler.

During recent weeks the war has reached a breath-taking
tempo - military and political. Events follow one another as
never before in war. Nowhere, however, has the enemy quite
been able to reach the speed for which the German offensive of
39-41 was distinguished, as compensation for this. The enemy
rolls forward simultaneously on all fronts, from the Atlantic to
the Far East, and from the Mediterranean to the Baltic. The
god of war has begun his spurt to the end.

Copied from the German News, Fallingbostol 3rd Sept.1944

To all prisoners of war - To escape from prison camps is no
longer a sport! Germany has always kept to the Hague

Convention, and only punished recaptured prisoners of war with minor disciplinary punishment. Germany will still maintain these principles of International Law, but England has, besides fighting at the front in an honest manner, instituted an illegal warfare in non-combat zones, in the form of Gangster Commandoes, Terror Bandits, and Sabotage Troops, even up to the frontiers of Germany.

They say, in a captured secret and confidential English military pamphlet - The Handbook of Modern Iregular Warfare - the days when we could practice the rules of sportsmanship are over. For the time being every soldier must be a potential Gangster, and must be able to adopt their methods whenever necessary. The sphere of operations should always include the enemy's own country, any occupied territory, and in certain circumstances such neutral country as he is using as a source of supply. England has, with these instructions,opened up a non-military form of gangster war. Germany is determined to safeguard her homeland, and especially her war industry and provision centres for the fighting fronts. Therefore it has become necessary to create strictly forbidden zones called Death Zones, in which all unauthorised trespassers will be immediately shot on sight. Escaping prisoners of war entering such Death Zones will certainly lose their lives. They are therefore in constant danger of being mistaken for enemy agents or Sabotage Groups. Urgent warning is given against making future escapes. In plain English - stay in the camps where you will be safe. Breaking out is now a damned dangerous act.

The chances of preserving your life are almost nil. All police and military guards have been given the most strict orders to shoot on sight all suspected persons. Escaping from prison camps has ceased to be a sport!

Our Camp Leader James A.G.Deans M.B.E. - While a P.O.W.

The name of Dixie Dean is remembered, in some awe and with abundant gratitude, by thousands of flying men who were taken prisoner, both in Britain and the Commonwealth. In post-war years he has been an honoured guest on many occasions in Canada, Australia, and New Zealand.

After he was shot down on his 25th Op.in September 1940, his personality as a leader quickly emerged, in a community composed of men who had been selected, in those early years of the war, for their resource and individuality. By common consent he was elected Camp Leader, and occupied this redoubtable position until 1945. Dixie was an NCO Whitley pilot. In the early stages he had under his   control and guidance a few hundred fellow prisoners. By the end of the war he was the trusted and respected guardian to several thousand. He was also in charge of the Escape Committee, the secret radio, and the Code, by which military secrets were relayed through letters to the British authorities. He was concerned with the increasing domestic problems of men whose wives had given up waiting and forsaken their marriage. He was in fact the buffer between the captors and the captives. He walked a delicate tightrope across perilous years. His safety net lay in the fact that the enemy recognised his inestimable worth as an "ambassador extraordinary". This mutual trust reached it's apex in the closing days of the war. The thousands of airmen, under Dixie's control, were marched eastwards from Stalag 357, Fallingbostol near Hanover, across the Elbe into Mecklenburg. By this time Germany was grinding to a halt, with the British and the Americans driving in from the west, and the Russians from the east.

In post-war years Dixie, still revered by men everywhere, was elected President of the Royal Air Force ex POW Association. His career blighted by multiple sclerosis, Dixie was in a wheel chair for some years, but with the help of his indomitable wife Molly he played an active part in the affairs of the Association. Now that Dixie has passed away he is sadly missed. His capacity to inspire men, some in high positions, is undiminished.

Don London   Hon.Sec. POW Association

DIXIE DEAN
in 1970.
Lower photograph taken in a POW
camp some time after being
shot down in 1940.

Letter from Mr Mottershead in charge of the 158 Squadron Club.

Dear Sir,

Many thanks for your enquiry on the reunion of 158 Squadron. It is always nice to hear of 158 types, and although we know the whereabouts of some 400 or so, each year, like yourself, a few more get to hear about us and turn up. It is nice to know that people are still keen enough to learn about those they knew almost 40 years ago.

From my book of crews I see your crew as follows:-

Pilot   W/O A.R.Van Slyke R.C.A.F   R121701
Navigator   P/O A.McGillivary R.C.A.F.   J20232
Bomb-Aimer F/Sgt.J.N.A.McDonagh R.C.A.F   139235
Wop/Ag   Sgt.H.Ball   1435132
Mid Upper Gunner Sgt.V.R.Grant   1822923
Rear Gunner   Sgt.K.D.Marsden-Mowbray 1323693
F/gt Engineer   Sgt.R.Whitelaw   1562120

Unfortunately although, as I have said, we know where a lot of 158 bods are, I do not know the present addresses of any of your crew - you are the first to contact us. If, however, you know of any, will you let me know so that I can send them a copy of the reunion gen. If I hear from any of your crew in the future I will pass them on to you. We normally hold reunions once a year, and as you will see the 1983 reunion will be in Bridlington. The 1984 venue has yet to be arranged.

My Wop was Chick McKinnon, and would still have been at Lissett when you arrived. I finished my tour in December 1943 with a trip to Berlin. S/Ldr.Sandy Sandall who was the Signals Officer at that time, and whom you probably knew, attends every reunion, and will be at Brize Norton this time.

If I can be of further assistance to you, please do not hesitate to contact me and I will help if I can.

As a point of interest, which POW camps were you in? We have a number of ex-POWs who come to the reunions. Also please can I have your Christian name, and if you can remember any of your crew's Christian names it would help.

Sincerely yours

Bluey
H. N. Mottershead

MR MOTTERSHEAD in charge of 158 Squadron Association
Sandy Sandell, my war-time signals leader
is on his left, bare-headed.
Taken at a 158 Reunion at Bridlington

German Communique 24th March 1944

Over 2000 tons of bombs on Berlin last night. More than 1000 planes sent. 73 aircraft missing".

Radio Luxemburg this afternoon - "Owing to the approach of enemy planes, Radio Luxemburg is going off the air".

Earlier today German radio reported "Single enemy planes are over Central Germany".

Official news of the great night raid on Berlin by the RAF is given in the following Air Ministry communique - "Last night Bomber Command dispatched over 1000 aircraft. Berlin was the main target, and more than 2500 tons of H.E. and incendiary bombs were dropped on industrial areas of the capital. First reports indicate that the attack was concentrated and that large fires were left burning. Other aircraft bombed objectives in Kiel and Western Germany". Today's German communique claimed that - " In the course of a renewed terror attack on the German capital during last night, the British raiders suffered extremely heavy losses - 112 four-engined bombers were destroyed.

20 mile Searchlight Belt

"A very large force of Lancasters and Halifax's dropped 2500 tons of H.E. and incendiary bombs on Berlin" states Air Ministry News Service.

One Lancaster pilot said of the German defences " Last night they put everything they had into it. The flack was heavier than I've known it, and it seemed that they must have used every searchlight they could get their hands on. There was one belt which appeared to stretch for 20 miles, and I saw one of our bombers twisting and turning to get out of the beams. It was a long time before they escaped"

Introduction to Five True Short Stories.

As I have written my first book as an autobiography, so much of my story was included in that book. With the best of my ability I am trying to make my second book a little different. The aircrew in these stories have one thing in common - they were all shot down in a raid on Berlin, four directly over the target, and two on their way home. Four flew in Halifax's and two in Lancasters. (The Halifax's were from 158 Squadron Lissett.) Two were shot down on 31st August 1943, and four on 24th March 1944 - the same night as the Great Escape when 50 RAF officers were shot by the S.S. In each case the planes were attacked by Junkers 88, German night fighters. Five of the aircrew were made prisoners of war, and one managed to evade capture. Of the rest of their crews, quite a few were killed in each aircraft, and almost all were wounded. In my own crew three went down with the aircraft.

Some of the authors have given me permission to use their stories, others I have not been able to contact. To them I apologise for using part of their story. In telling these stories I feel that it is my story as well. They give an insight into the lives of thousands of British and Commonwealth flyers who took off from Yorkshire aerodromes during the war. Only a small minority lived to tell the tale. Most of these came from crews operating during the last years of the war, when the Allied Forces in the air had the upper hand. Most of the aircrew who were shot down and taken prisoner survived the war, although some were badly wounded. Halifax bombers suffered higher casualties than the more manoeuverable Lancasters, and the official history shows the number of Halifax crews surviving 30 operations in 1942,'43 and the beginning of 1944 fluctuating between 2.6 per cent and 8 per cent. The youngsters who made up the wartime aircrews that flew our heavy bombers from Yorkshire and Lancashire bases came from widely different backgrounds, but their common experience of running the nightly gauntlet of night fighters, flack, and searchlights created a bond between them which transcended all social and national barriers within the Commonwealth. For the minority who survived, the youngest of them now in their 70s and 80s, this spirit of camaraderie is still very much alive, and finds practical expression in the activities of the Aircrew Association and the RAF clubs.
Ex POW W/O H.Ball 1435132
my part of the story has already been written.

WARRANT

The Right Honourable the SECRETARY OF STATE FOR AIR

To   _Harry Batt_

By virtue of the Authority to me, by the King's Most Excellent Majesty in this behalf given.

I do hereby Constitute and Appoint you to be a Warrant Officer in His Majesty's
Royal Air Force   from the _Thirtieth_
day of _April_   19 45 , and to continue in the said Office during the pleasure of the
Right Honourable the Secretary of State for Air.   You are therefore carefully and diligently to
discharge your Duty as such by doing and performing all manner of things thereunto belonging, as
required by the Established Regulations of the Service, and you are to observe and follow such Orders
and Directions as you shall receive from your Commanding, or any other, your superior Officer,
according to the Rules and Discipline of War.

GIVEN under my Hand and Seal of the Air Council this _Thirtieth_
day of _May 1945_

The second story is by my own navigator Allan McGillivary, Canadian. This is his own story, told after baling out of a stricken Halifax bomber, over the target, on a raid on Berlin on 24th March 1944, starting with the aircraft out of control, and the navigator trying to get the front hatch open:-

After two attacks by a Junkers 88, the aircraft was on fire and completely out of control, going down in a spin. I was trying to get the front hatch open, as well as putting on my parachute, with difficulty. When the hatch opened up I stuck my feet through the hole and the slipstream did the rest. The next thing I can remember is realising that my chute had opened and I was floating down into the heart of enemy territory, and no sign of the aircraft anywhere. Strangely the first thing that came into my mind was the thought that I wouldn't be getting back to Base. Then of course I began to wonder what would become of me when I landed in enemy territory. The air was desperately cold, and I seemed to take a long time to get down. The night was pitch black and I kept looking to see what kind of landscape I was coming down into. Suddenly I hit something. I didn't know what it was until the chute began dragging me along the ground. I had landed in a hayfield, and there were little stacks of hay here and there. I grabbed my chute and stuffed it under a pile of hay. Then what to do? I had lost my sense of direction, and although I could tell by the stars which was North, it seemed like it was South, and it remained like that all the while I was in Germany.

Escape seemed impossible, but we were supposed to try, so I decided to head North as Denmark and Sweden were probably the best bet, I started walking along the edge of a large drainage ditch, and had not gone far when I saw something white down in the ditch. When I got closer I saw that it was McDonagh (bomb aimer) lying there. His ankle had been badly mangled from the canon shells and he was unable to walk, and so had remained where he landed. He claimed that he would be alright and that I should leave him, since my chances of escape were probably nil anyway, and in the dark we couldn't tell what the wounds were like. I covered him up with his parachute, and set off along the ditch. I thought I had seen a light on the other side of the bridge, so I crossed it and continued on down the road. Soon I saw that I was approaching a village. I wondered what kind of a reception I was going to get. Seeing no alternative, I went up to the first house. No luck there so I went to the next one. Eventually someone came , and said something through an opening at the side of the door. I didn't know any German but tried to let them know who I was by saying "Canada" a few times. I don't know whether I got through to them or not, but they slammed the little door shut and that was that. It was the same story wherever I stopped, until finally I got near to the centre of the village and met a guy coming rather unsteadliy down the street. He turned out to be a German soldier, apparently making his way back to barracks after a night out. I don't think he knew who I really was , but he took me along to his sleeping quarters, where I soon became the centre of attention of every pair of eyes in the place.

After a short discussion, a couple of them took me over to the Burgermeister's house, which was only a short distance away. They got him out of bed, and I tried again to make him understand what I wanted. By then they had decided who and what I was. The Burgermeister's wife, who had arrived on the scene, went to wake her daughter who had apparently been taking English lessons at school. She was only ten or twelve years old, but was able to understand what I wanted. However it became apparent that nothing could be done until the Military Commander arrived.

I was given a basin of water and told to go and use it. When I saw myself in the mirror I could see why ! Apparently the blood from my temple had been running down the side of my face and freezing while I was coming down with the chute, and now it was a great bloody clot, and a sight to behold. After I had cleaned myself as well as I could, this good kind lady came with antiseptic and a clean cloth and bandaged me up as nice as could be.

It was getting daylight before the Commandant came along, but when he found out the situation he quickly rounded up six men and a stretcher, and set out to rescue McDonagh. He was where I had left him, and was soon on his way on the stretcher. Another surprise when we got back to the house was that this good housewife had got two of her neighbours over, and they were in Red Cross uniforms, and with First Aid equipment ready to do what they could for Mac. Late in the afternoon a van arrived and we were loaded up, and started on the first leg of our trip to a POW camp. With several others we were picked up and put on a train for Frankfurt Interrogation Centre. McDonagh was then taken to a Berlin hospital. Being an officer, I was sent to an officers' camp - Stalagluft 1 - where I remained until I was released at the end of the war.

Allan McGillivary

*I was only
inspecting the
drains !*

Tunnels were usually started from the billets or wash-houses, these offering good cover for the entrance.

Some of the most successful, however, were started in the open. In one instance the entrance trap-door was situated in the centre of a garden and supported some very fine lettuce.

McGillivary was my navigator in Van Slyke's crew, flying Halifax's at 158 Squadron Lissett. McDonagh was my bomb aimer.

Air Gunner/Wireless Operator Ron Thurston from 158 Squadron.

His experiences of baling out over Berlin, written and explained much better than I could.

Baling out of a blazing bomber over Berlin, one of the most heavily defended cities in Germany, could possibly be described as "baling out of Hell into Hell", as I experienced at midnight on 31st August 1943, when a Halifax bomber of 158 Squadron Lissett, in which I was flying as a Wireless-Airgunner, was attacked directly over the target by enemy night fighters, seconds after the bombs were dropped and immediately after the bomb doors closed. Seconds earlier and the whole crew would have perished, instead of just three. No evasive action can possibly be carried out on a bombing run. To bale out of a blazing bomber, still under attack, with two engines on fire, completely out of control, coned by the searchlights, amongst over 600 other bombers dropping bombs from various heights, night fighters, flares, and bursting shells from anti-aircraft guns certainly concentrates the mind. Then the parachute opened and gently drifted away from the nightmare.

Thoughts in the dark - the dangerous sky, and the fate of the rest of the crew. How many had been killed in this Hell? You look around in the darkness for parachutes, and see nothing. The searchlights sweep the sky as if looking for you, assisting the night fighters in their attack. You watch, with fascination, the blazing target, the explosions of the bombs, and the retaliation of the anti-aircraft guns, with little thought of the danger of the thousands of bits of flack in the air. You wonder if the tracer bullets you see are coming from an air-gunner's turret, or from an enemy fighter attacking one of our bombers. You watch with dismay a blazing bomber plunging to earth, and wonder if anyone got out. Your parachute seems to be going up instead of coming down, and you feel slightly sick from the swaying. You begin to wonder what your height is when you see a night fighter only a little way above you, and when and where you will land. Will you be shot when in the hands of the enemy? or shown mercy as a POW? All these thoughts as you slowly, alone and completely helpless, descend into the unknown. Your face feels wet with perspiration - or is it raining? You feel a little numb in this dark unreal world, and wonder if you are dreaming. The crunch of an anti-aircraft shell nearby, as the bombing continues, reminds you that you aren't. You listen to the humming engines of the bombers - some will be shot down on the way home, perhaps over the sea. All the way back to the English coast, and sometimes inland, they will be pursued by determined enemy night fighters, with their excellent radar and brave pilots, eager to be credited with the destruction of another bomber. The bomber crews are alert to all this, and do not relax for one moment. As you are mesmerised by the red glow in the sky from the fires, observing the flashes from the anti-aircraft guns, and the shell-bursts in the sky, you begin to think of your loved ones at home. In a few hours they will receive that dreaded telegram, which they have been half expecting ever since you started operational flying - "Regret to inform you that your . . . . . "(I still have mine), and you begin to wonder when, and if, you will ever see them again.

Ron Thurston

Michael's Story

This is another story of a Berlin raid on 24th March 1944. The crew member was Michael Baldwin, a wireless air-gunner in a Lancaster bomber, and the story is told by himself.

At 21hrs on the night of 24th March 1944, our Lancaster "K" for king took off from our base at RAF Witchford near Ely, fully laden with an 8000lb bomb and incendiaries, on our trip to Berlin. This was a "big-un" and maximum effort with well over 1000 aircraft, and many diversions to lesser targets.

We were due over Berlin in the first wave at about 11.15pm, and it was one hell of a cold night. We crossed the coast at Cromer, and turned on a long leg up the North Sea to Sylt, climbing on track. We crossed over Sylt and turned on course east to Stettin and on to Berlin. Over Sylt I saw two planes go down in flames. We settled down to the job in hand. We turned again on track to cross Berlin from north-east to south-west. Berlin is a big city, spread out over a large area. We were early over the target. Anti-aircraft shells were exploding well below us - a sure sign of night fighters at our height. We saw the p.p.f. markers go down, and headed on to our point, dropping our bombs on given time. We headed for home, crossing the Ruhr well north near Hanover, across Holland and back to base. That all sounds very ordinary but .....we were attacked, according to our rear gunner, by a Junkers 88 who split us open with his canon shells. I was listening to a Group broadcast at the time, and as I switched over my intercom I heard the dreaded words "Adandon aircraft". I forgot to unplug my headset and nearly pulled my head off. I moved to the rear to find the exit and opened the door behind me - the whole area was one huge mass of flames, bright orange and hot. I closed the door and went forward. I had automatically taken my parachute from it's stowage and clipped it on my harness.

The aircraft was now performing the most weird acrobatics, and I found myself literally stuck to the ceiling by the force of "G". No panic, but how the hell do I get out? At that moment my problem was solved. The aircraft literally broke in half, and out I went into the dark unknown. I obviously missed the fixed-wire aerial and the trailing aerial, and I lapsed into unconsciousness through lack of oxygen and the intense cold.

I came to my senses, and found that I was falling through the dark night. All was completely quiet. I went to pull my parachute handle and then panicked - it wasn't there! I was falling in a straight position, and when I looked up I noticed that my chute was flapping unopened above me on the ends of my harness webbing. I couldn't reach it. I pulled the harness down towards me, found my chute and pulled the handle. It plopped open straight away, and I realised that my heart-beat was, to say the least, very fast. I landed on the top of a huge forest fir tree, and found that I was tangled up in the branches and shroud. I realised that my chute had opened with only seconds to spare, and before it could slow my descent, I hit the tree at well over 100 miles per hour. I swung towards a decent sized branch, unclipped my release, and started to climb down the tree. I wasn't apparently injured. I reached the bottom branch of the tree and saw snow beneath me - about a six foot drop. I jumped and found that I had landed in snow about six feet deep. I took stock of myself and realised that I was bare-footed - my flying boots and socks had been ripped off. I had a packet of cigarettes and an orange in my flying blouse. The juice of the orange had soaked into the cigarettes turning them into a handful of soggy tobacco. I succeeded in finding a forest look-out post, about 75ft high with a ladder, and I climbed up to see just where I was. All I could see in the moonlight were thousands of huge trees as far as the eye could see, and I could hear the sounds of aircraft above, all heading for home.

Michael Baldwin

Harry's Story

Harry Simister was another member of a crew from 158 Squadron Lissett who was shot down over Berlin on 31st August 1943. They were in a Halifax bomber when they were attacked by German night fighters, probably Junkers 88s. The port engines were knocked out and on fire, and the fuselage was set ablaze. The plane was completely out of control and went into a spin. Flight Engineer Harry Simister followed the wireless operator, bomb aimer, and navigator through the hatch. He had not adjusted his harness properly, and felt a terrific pull on his legs as he fell through space. His parachute eventually opened. It was very cold. He was being blown away from the target which was a mass of flames. (The same thing happened to me). He hit the ground, as he described it, like a wet a sack. (The same happened to me, but I landed in a dyke). Harry had been wounded in the aircraft - he could feel the wetness inside his shirt and trousers, where his wounds were still bleeding. Because of the numbness and shock it didn't hurt much. He covered his chute with tufts of grass, then lay down and tried to get some sleep. Now in Harry's case he was determined not to get caught, and he managed to evade capture for one year and ten days. He was a very special person, but he must have had lots of luck. He travelled through a lot of countries before he got back to England. The route he took was from Brussels through France to Switzerland. In October 1943 he could have seen out the war, but instead he escaped into France with another RAF chap and joined the Maquis. He then went to Naples and found the British Army, and then flew to Tunis, Algiers, Oran and Casablanca, before arriving back at St.Eval Cornwall in a Coastal Command plane.

I have not gone into any real detail in this short story, because it is his to tell, not mine.

Harry Simister was awarded the Military Medal.

" *I've just made you a brew on the ' Smokeless Wonder ' ! *"

Alkemade

This is the part of his story that I was interested in. He was later caught and sent to the Interrogation Centre at Frankfurt, and then on to a POW camp - more than likely the same camp that I was in.

Here is another unusual story about a gunner in a Lancaster bomber who was shot down on the same night as myself, 24th March 1944. His name was S Alkemade.

Where we were caught over the target, they were caught on the way home, and Alkemade was wounded. Four of the crew died in the aircraft when it exploded. Three of my crew died in the same way when our plane crashed.

What I went through was tame compared with Alkemade's experiences. I am not going to poach his story, but it was similar to what happened to my crew. When his pilot gave the order to abandon ship, everyone capable went to put on his parachute, but when Alkemade went to collect his chute, which was behind him in the aircraft, to his dismay it was on fire and was of no use to him.By now the whole plane was on fire, and was liable to explode at any moment. He had to make a decision - whether to burn to death in the aircraft, or die quickly when he jumped out and hit the ground. He chose to jump out!

At first he didn't feel as if he was falling, and could see stars below him. It was obvious - he was upside down. Then he lost consciousness, from shock or maybe lack of oxygen. The plane had been flying at about 18,000ft, and at over 10,000ft you could easily pass out or get frostbite. He woke up lying in the underbrush and snow. It was very cold and his back and legs were giving him a lot of pain. After moving about a bit he realised that he was all in one piece. He must have hit the ground at a speed of well over 100 miles per hour, and it was only the soft branches of the trees and the snow that had saved his life. He lost his flying boots in the fall,and his clothes were scorched. Later when he was taken prisoner and sent to a POW camp, it came as a relief after what he had been through.He was taken to a hospital - probably the same one in Berlin as my bomb aimer went to - and in the operating theatre the doctor found that he had burnt legs, a twisted right knee, a deep splinter wound in his thigh. strained back, slight concussion, a scalp wound, and various degrees of burns on his face and hands. Most of the damage was done in the aircraft. After treatment he was sent to Frankfurt Interrogation Centre. The Germans didn't believe him at first when he told them that he had baled out at 18,00ft without a parachute - they thought that he was trying to make fools of them. However, when he told them where the aircraft had crashed, the Germans searched the plane and found the remains of his parachute. Eventually they believed him and went to the trouble of corroborating his story in writing, saying that Sgt.Alkemade was truthful in all repects, and this was witnessed by Senior British Officers.

I never met the chap, but it is highly likely that we travelled in the same cattle trucks through Poland to Heydekrug in East Prussia, and we were probably in the same camps - Heydekrug, Thorn, and Fallingbostol (nicknamed the Kriegi Run). Even our Service numbers were similar. Sgt.Alkemade lost four of his crew, I lost two on my first trip and three on my last trip to Berlin.

I was the only member of our crew to come out of the war without a scratch. I must have had a guardian angel.

Roy Child

This is a story, again very similar to my own, about Roy Child, Air Gunner and POW from 1944 - 45.

On 20th February 1944 Roy's aircraft was shot down on a trip to Leipzig by a Junkers 88. Three of the crew were killed in the aircraft, and four were taken prisoner - exactly the same as our crew. Roy was taken to Frankfurt Interrogation Centre, and then on the same route as myself, travelling by cattle truck to Heydekrug in East Prussia, Thorn in Poland, and Fallingbostol in Germany. Then in the last month of the war, on a forced march, we were most likely in the same column which was attacked by RAF Typhoons, with disastrous results. He was wounded in one leg. Although I was in the middle of it I got off scot-free.

Roy Child wrote a book called "A Wartime Log". In August 1985 I bought a copy of his book and he very kindly wrote in it - *To H. Ball who shared those years with me* and then signed it. I thought that was very nice of him.

It is surprising, when you think of it, that 12,000 POWs were roaming around Germany at the end of the war, and stories are still being written about their experiences. I am writing about just a few.

This is a letter from a navigator, George Barrett, who was with 158 Squadron at the same time as myself. He was shot down in February 1944 (a month before me). All his crew were killed. He was lucky to get out alive, although he was wounded.

Dear Harry,
Yes, I was pleased to hear from you yesterday. I forwarded your name and address to Ken Holmes our membership secretary last night, and you will no doubt receive a membership form within the next day or two, I hope!

The White Rose branch of the A.C.A. is quite active. It is now in it's third year, and amongst the 90 or so members, we have people from Ripon, Catterick, Leeds and Selby. I personally do not help a lot in the promoting of it's events, because I am, with three others, on the 4 Group Reunion Committee. Every other year in York the 4 Group Reunions attract 380 people, this number being the most we can cope with for the catering. Last year we had people from America, Australia, New Zealand, France and Norway. 158 Squadron had a couple of dozen at their table. A couple of years ago the BBC covered the activities of the Committee and the events of the weekend. I mentioned 158 in that particular programme - perhaps you saw it, it was shown a couple of times. It was not until 1980 that I had the pleasure of meeting someone from 158 - a chap by the name of Pete Skinner.

In Heydekrug I was in D12, and worked with Dickie Pape on the production of the Evening News. I drew up the heads for him. I met an ex-Heydekrug chap last year by the name of Ginger Furze. We had quite a long chat.

Whilst at Lissett I flew with Penfold, an Australian called Simpson, and my regular crew skippered W.Holmes. Our W/op was a Newcastle lad called Tony Rogerson.

The book "In Great Company" makes no mention of us apart from 6k.1.POW February 19-20 1944 at the back of the book. Bill Chorley did a lot of research for me a few years ago. I lost my log book , so he was good enough to search through Squadron records to see which trips I had been on.

I look forward to meeting you one of these days. In the meantime, Harry, all the best.

George Barrett
Good old 158

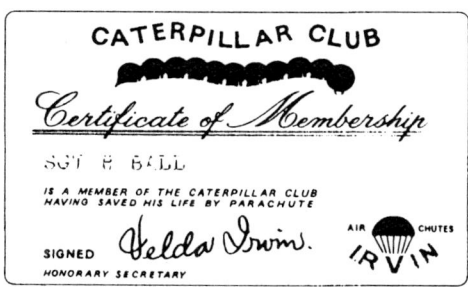

POETRY

In this book I write mostly about myself and the RAF. When we left Poland we were taken to Fallingbostal in Germany, to an Army POW camp. (Almost straight away our camp leader Dixie Dean took over the camp). Mixing with the Army gave us the chance to swop stories about our experiences. From these meetings I picked up poems, mainly about the fighting in the desert, which I published in my first book. Here is one very special poem which I must repeat.

Requiem for a Rear Gunner
By R.W.Gilbert

Dedicated to my old "opo" Sid Fox, late of 158 Squadron, 4 Group, Bomber Command, and all those thousands of fresh-faced youngsters who got the chop whilst on ops. in the dark and hostile night skies over occupied Europe 1939-1945. We have not forgotten you.

The last time I saw Paris, her heart was far from gay.
Ten thousand feet below us, the sleeping city lay.
The sky was filled with aircraft. The moon was big and bright.
Two hundred heavy bombers were winging through the night.

We'd left our Yorkshire airfield at Lissett on the Moor,
at half-past ten that evening in 1944.
The briefing room had echoed with banter and with scorn,
We're only off to Paris, we'll be back before the dawn.

No ribbon stretched menacingly to Essen or Berlin.
The red line crossed the Channel and ended on the Seine.
This ought to be a piece of cake, with little flak to face,
and ere the fighters know we're there, we'll all be back to base.

We'd had our eggs and bacon, our usual pre-op meal.
As each one hid with nervous smiles, the fear we all must feel.
We'd drawn our flying rations, our Mae Wests and our chutes.
We'd togged up in our bulky gear - long socks and flying boots.

Around the dark perimeter the squadron buses run,
with dully glowing headlamps, blacked out to foil the Hun.
Like Mayfair cruising taxis they trundle through the murk,
Taking the restless aircrews out, to their evening's work.

Driven by young and pretty WAAFs, who make our spirits soar,
They drop us at Dispersal and then return for more.
The ground crew have been working since early in the day,
To have our aircraft ready, our faithful X X-ray.

In black and dark green camouflage, our Halifax stands there,
Like some great pondering bird of prey, eager to take the air.
We climb aboard together, to check our charts and gear,
To give a final polish to turrets mid and rear.

We smoke another Woodbine, the last one of the day.
"We'll see you in the morning", we hear the ground staff say.
The skipper starts the engines, and runs them up all four.
The mighty Hercules motors give a powerful roar.

The oxygen is tested, we try the intercom,
although we won't need oxygen from the height we're due to
bomb.
We join our queueing comrades, lined up around the track.
We know we're now committed, there'll be no turning back.

Already "A" for Apple, and "B" for Baker too,
have rumbled down the runway, to vanish in the blue.
The sun is almost setting, our take off time is near.
We reach the glass control tower, a crowd has gathered here.

We turn on to the runway, and watch the Aldis glow,
of twenty laden aircraft, we are the last to go.
A "green" gives us permission, the runway now is free,
We're flying off to Paris, to see what we can see.

The Groupie and the Wing Co have been here for half an hour,
The Skipper gives a "thumbs up", acknowledged by the tower.
Some sad WAAFs stand silent, their hearts are cold with fear,
Their eyes are focused skywards, on someone they hold dear.

The fire crew and the blood tub have everyone in check,
in case we burst a tyre, and fail to leave the deck.
We thunder down the tarmac, the wheels are racing fast,
Our Halifax is lifting, airborne we are at last.

Circling around the airfield, we slowly gain some height,
The navigator gives a course, we head South through the night.
We keep on climbing gently, till at six thousand feet,
when flying straight and level, our Squadron planes we meet.

And soon we're joined by dozens, like tiddlers in a pool,
We cross the River Humber, change course again at Goole.
Quite soon we're over Lincoln, six thousand feet below,
crossing the "Five Group" airfields, with Lancs all set to go.

Tonight they won't be with us, as on and on we drone,
They'll find some other targets, - we'll do this one alone.
The heavens grow slowly darker, the moon is still asleep,
The gunners in their turrets a lonely vigil keep.

Two hundred fresh-faced pilots stare out with straining eyes,
watching for other bombers, though still in friendly skies.
Two hundred Halifax's are droning on unseen,
their tracks betrayed by nav lights of white and red and green.

Quite soon we reach the Channel, white cliffs beneath our
wings,
Out go those tell-tale nav lights, we think of many things.
The phosphorescent breakers glow silvery and gold,
We see the moon is rising, the summer night grows cold.

The gunners search increasingly, no-one can take a chance,
We climb up to ten thousand, and cross the coast of France.
Now several probing searchlights reach skyward for the pack,
while from Boulogne's defences come many bursts of flak.

That silvery winding ribbon, etched white across the plain,
is France's noble waterway, the widely flowing Seine.
Her bridges now in ruins, her river boats no more
sail out from Paris playgrounds to Le Havre's distant shore.

Touching the edge of Normandy, by Rouen's ancient wall,
the enslaved sleeping populace are waiting freedom's call.
In their uneasy slumbers, how little do they know?
The landings on the beaches have just three dawns to go.

Some kilometres westward the "D Day" bells will chime,
as up the fire-raked beaches the Allied soldiers climb.
Through searing shell and bomb burst, to face the evil Hun,
to fight their bloody battles, till victory is won.

The gunners in their turrets, at mid-upper and at rear,
increase the frantic searching, as zero hour draws near.
The pilots in their cock-pits fly on with pounding hearts,
while lonely navigators pore over dim lit charts.

Bomb aimers lying prostrate, gaze fervently below,
approaching Paris environs, they watch the city grow.
The wireless operators sit listening to their sets,
flight engineers attending to petrol cocks and jets.

This is the sort of target we picture in our dreams,
No crashing, blinding flak burst, no packs of Huns, it seems.
No Dante's fire like Dusseldorf, and Essen in the Ruhr,
No desperate trip like Nuremberg, when we lost ninety-four.

The Skipper breaks the silence, three minutes now to go,
Pathfinder markers falling, on railway sheds below.
Suspended in the moonlight, long beads of green and red,
all interspersed with flashes of brilliant flares ahead.

With bomb doors gaping open, we steadily press on,
till Larry's voice announces "Left, left a bit - BOMBS GONE"!
The Skipper shoves the nose down, out and away we go,
as smoke and flames gush skyward from the doomed yards
below.

I feel relieved and happy, the moon is on our beam,
Then suddenly the fighters are in amongst the stream.
Combat breaks out on every side, the criss-cross bullets fly,
I see four stricken bombers fall blazing from the sky.

As cannon shells come leaping, I watch the battle grow,
A Halifax to starboard attacks a One-one-o.
I see another aircraft about to meet it's fate,
A fighter closes in on him, a JU-88.

This is is no even contest, no warring of the gods,
Our bullets can't match cannon shells, we know the desperate odds.
I nurse my four sleek Brownings, with their belts of 303,
and hold them on the 88, that's quietly shadowing me.

With twice our speed, he's half our size, we're lucky to survive,
The only thing that we can do is weave and twist and dive.
He takes a chancy pot-shot, his shells fall short astern,
He's just a bit too eager to see our aircraft burn.

I tell the Skip to corkscrew before we get the chop,
and as we're diving steeply, I watch the fighter drop.
He very quickly vanishes into the hazy air,
and then with startling suddenness he fires a fighter flare.

Suspended on a parachute it hangs above our tail,
glowing with brilliant radiance, making the moon seem pale.
Crouched in my rear turret, well, how am I to know
that the cunning Hun is waiting, a hundred feet below.

We have no under-turret, no-one can see below,
He sits there as we corkscrew, following as we go.
An upward firing cannon, close by the pilot's cheek,
is beaded on my turret, it's code name "Schrage Musik".

Where ignorance is bliss, they say, 'tis folly to be wise,
though soon I'll face the music in those unfriendky skies.
We have the flare behind us, suspended there on high,
I watch it fading slowly, from the corner of my eye.

Once more the sky is empty, so peaceful and unreal,
I call through on the intercom "Regain an even keel -
You can straighten up now Skipper, we've lost him I believe,
but don't fly straight and level, maintain a gentle weave".

No sign of JU-88s, no ME-One-one-o's,
Quite soon now we'll be at the coast, where the English Channel flows.
I sigh and breathe in deeply, with ill-disguised relief . . .
when streams of white hot tracer come hosing from beneath.

My world dissolves around me, I take a fearful blow,
My legs are ripped and shattered from that holocaust below.
My Browning guns have vanished, my chest is torn and red,
my perspex dome disintegrates - I am already dead!

Epitaph
My brief, sweet life is over, my eyes no longer see,
No summer walks, no Christmas trees, no pretty girls for me.
I've got the chop, I've had it, my nightly ops are done,
Yet in another hundred years - I'll still be twenty-one.

Three episodes connected with the RAF, by H.Ball

In 1984 I retired from business and my wife and I decided to tour Scotland, and see if we could find my mid-upper gunner Grant who lived in Elgin, near Lossiemouth where we were stationed during the war. We stopped off at Perth, and stayed overnight at a cottage for "bed and breakfast". While talking to the landlady about our main reason for coming to Scotland, she surprised me by saying that her husband flew in Halifax's during the war, and was on special duties at a secret station near York. He was in the Caterpillar Club, and he also had a Goldfish badge for being rescued at sea in a dinghy. I told her about all the clubs I had joined, and the famous people I had met, and that I had taken a photograph of Bill Reid VC. To my surprise she said "My husband is out playing golf with him now!" However, I didn't get the chance to see him again.

We eventually met up with Grant through one of his daughters who worked at a supermarket in Elgin. He had retired after being a Chief Inspector of Police in Manchester for 31 years.

McGillivary our navigator, who lived in Canada, had not seen Grant (one of our gunners) since the end of the war, so he asked me if I could somehow arrange a meeting. In 1985 (Ithink) McGillivary wrote and said that he was coming over to England for a holiday, and could Grant and I meet him at the London Hilton. I arranged for Grant and his wife to come and stay with us overnight in Harrogate, and then I would drive them down to London. The six of us met at the hotel and had a meal. I suppose it was a bit boring for the wives, but the three of us really enjoyed ourselves. On the way home Grant said that although it had been a long way to travel, it was well worth it.

Grant died of a massive stroke a few years later.

In November 1994 a Mr Greenaway, who lived in my home town of Harrogate, died when he was out walking, at the age of 79. He had been a POW at Stalagluft 3, Sargon when the Great Escape took place. (A film was made of it in 1963). I met Mr Greenaway at the RAFA Club in Harrogate. He was giving a lecture on the same subject. When he had finished I went over and introduced myself.

He was wearing a POW tie like mine. I told him that I had been shot down over Berlin on the same night as the Great Escape, 24/25th March. All of a sudden he grabbed me by the coat and said "So you were one of them who caused the escape to be a failure". (He was kidding, of course). However, he could possibly have been right. Because of the big 1000 bomber raid on Berlin, all the lights went out, including in the tunnel where the men were trying to escape, and because the lights failed, more German guards were put on duty patrolling outside the wire. One of the Germans spotted an airman coming out of the tunnel, and that was that. Well over 100 were caught in the tunnel. Some had escaped, but I'm afraid that 50 were caught the next day, and were shot by S.S.troops.

Greenaway was a man of many talents. He was one of the chosen few who looked after the welfare of his fellow prisoners.He was in charge of the Secret Radio, and he forged the documents for those who wanted to escape. Also, being a cabinet maker, he did a lot of work in the Camp Theatre.

Finally, thank you for reading my book. Please do write to me with any information about 158 Squadron, or anything else you wish. If you do not know me personally and have my home address letters sent care of my publishers will soon reach me.

Harry Ball
Harrogate
August 1997

Appendix.

Summary of my Service life from 1941 to 1946.

The camps at which I was stationed - Training, Operational and POW.

Leeds - Recruiting Office. After my fifth try I was accepted.
Cardington - Medical for aircrew and basic training.
Blackpool - Footslogging, Wireless and Morse Code at 4 words a min.
Yatesbury - Wireless school and flying single-engined Proctor and twin-engined Dominie 1.
Feltwell - Operational squadron flying Wellingtons.
Mildenhall - Working with ground wireless mechanics.
Cranwell - No.1 Wireless School, maintenance course, and basic navigation.
Yatesbury - Refresher course. Passed out as Wireless Operator,
practical and theory. Morse Code up to 22 words per minute.
Manby - Gunnery School. Only there for a few days.
West Freugh - Gunnery course.
Stranraer - Flying twin-engined Ansons.
Lossiemouth - Operational training unit flying Wellingtons.
Elgin - Getting a full crew together.
Marston Moor - Conversion unit to 4-engined Halifax's.
Lissett - Operational squadron with full crew of 7, 158 Sqn.
Frankfurt, Germany - Interrogation Centre, Prisoner of War.
Heydekrug, East Prussia - Stalagluft 6, POW camp.
Thorn, Poland - POW camp
Fallingbostal, Germany - 357 Army camp, POW

The last month of the war, force marched. Living most of the time off the land, sleeping in barns, ditches, roadsides, farm sheds etc. Cosford - After being released by the Eighth Army, I was flown back to England in a Lancaster bomber. Cosford was a Receival and Disposal unit for POWs.

Missed V.E.Day and all the celebrations.
Church Fenton - Demob and postings
Redruth, Cornwall - Motor mechanic under training.
Stafford - No.16 Maintenance Unit from where I was demobbed.
Snaith - One night stop, due to aircraft collision.